# Meet Them Where They Are

*How connection and community will save us*
*...in business and beyond.*

**JENNIFER LYNNE CRONEBERGER**

Meet Them Where They Are
Copyright © 2025 by Jennifer Lynne Croneberger. All rights reserved.

No part of this book may be used or reproduced in any manner whatsoever without written permission, except in the case of brief quotations embodied in critical articles and reviews. For more information, e-mail all inquiries to info@mindstirmedia.com.

**MINDSTIR MEDIA**

Published by MindStir Media, LLC
45 Lafayette Rd | Suite 181| North Hampton, NH 03862 | USA
1.800.767.0531 | www.mindstirmedia.com

Printed in the United States of America.
ISBN-13: 978-1-965340-75-2

# CONTENTS

Foreword .................................................................................................. V
**Part I** ..................................................................................................... 1
Introduction ........................................................................................... 3
Chapter 1: How did we get here? ........................................................ 13
Chapter 2: Connection in a Disconnected World ............................. 21
Chapter 3: Be Where Your Feet Are .................................................... 33
Chapter 4: A Culture Defined by Work .............................................. 47
Chapter 5: The Magic of Building Relationships ............................. 57
Chapter 6: The Compelling Case for Compassion ........................... 65
Chapter 7: Through Broken Pieces We Mend ................................... 73

**Part II** .................................................................................................. 83
Chapter 8: B.R.A.V.E. and the Five Words ........................................ 85
Chapter 9: Belonging ........................................................................... 93
Chapter 10: Resilience ........................................................................ 107
Chapter 11: Authenticity ................................................................... 119
Chapter 12: Vulnerability ................................................................. 129
Chapter 13: Empathy ......................................................................... 141

**Part III** ............................................................................................... 159
Chapter 14: Where We Go From Here ............................................ 161
Chapter 15: How B.R.A.V.E. Behaviors Dictate Performance ...... 167
Chapter 16: How B.R.A.V.E. Is Your Culture? ................................ 199
Endnotes ............................................................................................. 211

## FOREWORD
## BY KEVIN HARRINGTON

Original "Shark" from ABC's hit show *Shark Tank*
and Bestselling Author of *Mentor to Millions*

As a global investor and the pioneer of the infomercial industry, I've built my career on recognizing game-changing ideas and the visionaries behind them. Whether it's in business, leadership, or personal growth, success often comes down to one essential factor: connection. It's the foundation of every healthy partnership, every high-performing team, and every revolutionary idea that has ever truly taken off. And that's exactly why *Meet Them Where They Are* by Jennifer Lynne Croneberger is a must-read.

Jennifer has cracked the code on what it means to be an impactful leader in today's environment. Her book speaks to me for many reasons. She is not just covering management techniques or generic leadership jargon—she's diving deep into what truly drives performance, innovation, and culture: *human connection*. I've navigated many changes in the workplace dynamic over the last 40 years, from the local, corporate office atmosphere to working remotely worldwide. In a time when digital interactions often replace face-to-face conversations and companies struggle to build authentic workplace cultures, this book serves as a powerful reminder that relationships—real, meaningful relationships—are what fuel success.

The B.R.A.V.E. Human Leadership model that Jennifer presents is a game-changer. *Belonging, Resilience, Authenticity, Vulnerability, and Empathy*—these aren't just buzzwords; they're the blueprint for how to lead, inspire, and create thriving organizations. And Jennifer doesn't just theorize—she brings this to life through real-world examples, compelling research, and stories that will make you rethink everything you thought you knew about leadership.

As an entrepreneur and investor, I know that the most successful businesses aren't just built on innovative products or cutting-edge technology. They're built on people—on leaders who know how to *meet their teams where they are*, foster trust, and create cultures that empower everyone to perform at their best. That's why this book is so powerful. Whether you're a CEO, a startup founder, a coach, or someone looking to make a greater impact in your community, *Meet Them Where They Are* will challenge you to lead with more intention, more heart, and more purpose.

Jennifer reminds us that leadership isn't just about strategy; it's about humanity. And if there's one thing I know for sure, it's that the leaders who embrace this philosophy will be the ones who drive the biggest results—both in business and in life.

I encourage you to dive in, embrace the B.R.A.V.E. framework, and start leading in a way that truly transforms. Because in the end, success isn't just about what you achieve; it's about the impact you leave behind.

Let's get to work.

~**Kevin Harrington**

# PART I

# INTRODUCTION

*"We don't want anything too 'touchy-feely,"*
*she said. "Our people aren't really like that."*

It was an unusually hot and humid afternoon in mid-May, somewhere around 2012. I was standing in the back of an extra-large moving truck after emptying the last couple things that belonged to a friend, who was moving out of a space and a life that no longer served her. It was at that moment that my phone rang obtrusively loudly—the ringtone bouncing off of the walls of the almost empty truck. I fumbled quickly in my pocket to make it stop. It was my 3pm appointment. I had lost track of time.

On the other end of the phone was a woman who had just emailed me that morning about a speaking opportunity for her organization. I quickly realized my voice would also echo off of the walls of the truck so I jumped out of the back and quickly moved to the cab, shutting the door and window behind me.

"Hello, this is Jen." I tried to sound business-like, as if I was not in the middle of a street in a moving truck with sweat dripping down my chin onto the end of the phone.

"Jen?" she asked.

"Yes, this is Jen," I repeated.

"Hi, this is Linda. We made a time to talk today?"

Trying not to sound too eager, I cut her off only a little bit.

"YES! Hi Linda."

I paused, not sure really what to say next or who was going to lead the conversation. I mean, she emailed me so I knew she was looking for me to speak at her event, but at the same time I didn't really know how these calls went since I had only had a handful before this. I got quiet. Then I started to worry I was too quiet.

"So, I wanted to find out your fee and if you were available on July 12."

*"Shit,"* I stammered internally. She led with the fee. I hate talking about money. I didn't even know what she wanted yet. That's like going into a restaurant and asking the hostess what the bill is going to be before I have even been handed the menu.

"Ummm … I usually charge a thousand dollars, but whatever you need, I can make it work. I mean if that's too much. Or whatever..." My voice started to trail off. I was stuttering and somehow still talking. OMG! I was now yelling at myself to shut up in my head, hardly hearing if she had said anything yet.

"Uhh, ok. Let me see what we can make work. July 12? You're good?"

"YES." I didn't even look. I didn't imagine there was any reason to check. I was sure I had nothing going on that day or the day before or the day after.

When I was a new speaker, as many do, I would answer every email and every phone call ready to take the gig no matter the fee, the date, the time, the audience, the location. I wanted to speak and I would do it for next to nothing if I had to. This led to a growing speaking career and a slight case of exhaustion bordering on burnout, and a skillset I could use for the rest of my life.

"Ok, so I liked a few things I was reading on your website …"

I stopped listening. Back into my head I went. "Website? Oh no. Have I even updated that?" Holy crap, I have NO idea what she was reading from my website.

And then, as soon as we nailed down details and were about to hang up, she spoke those 13 words that changed the trajectory of my career, and maybe even my life, forever.

*"We don't want anything too 'touchy-feely,'"*
*"Our people aren't really like that."*

Pause.
Full stop.
Full.
Fucking.
Stop.

Here I was, full steam ahead into my speaking career. I would change lives. I was going to be the next Tony Robbins. Maybe Oprah would talk to me once I got my name out there. I had arrived. I had the attitude of, "Just hire me. You won't regret it. I know how to make people FEEL good." Even if I didn't know what to charge, and had a hard time some days believing I was worth what people would pay just to hear me talk, I knew that this was what I was supposed to be doing.

And then I actually heard her. Wait. Did she say, "Too touchy-feely?"

I paused. Hesitated. Probably even stammered a little. It was like turning the lens all the way to the right on a completely out of focus projector that just became crystal clear. I should say something. I spent the next few minutes trying to convince her I was not, in fact, too "touchy-feely" and that I would deliver something very business-like and devoid of emotion. I pictured men and women in business suits, wearing dignified glasses that made them look smart, taking notes with stern faces. You know, like robots.

Yes. I can speak to them. "I will just … change … everything," I thought out loud. Cut out the stories and the fun. I guess this is what it will take to speak at corporate events. And so, with that thought, I began to re-work my keynote. She hired me a day later in an email. And I started to second-guess what I had just done.

Changing my work would be, in essence, changing the very core of who I am. After years of working hard to find myself, to live authentically in every aspect of my existence, and teaching others to do the same, I felt that creating something that wasn't me would be missing the mark. I would be abandoning the very fabric of the work I was doing. After all, time and time again, I was told my greatest gift was my ability to connect with my audience. That conversation stuck with me for a long time. In many ways it became the catalyst for the work I started to do in the field of leadership. I wanted to study it. If it was out there, I wanted to learn and know it. I spent time going back through my master's program and all the work I did on understanding leadership and how it transcends through an organization and a team. I dug through countless hours of research and articles. I talked with people. I asked hard questions. And I read. *A lot*.

I completed a certification program in Sustainable Business Strategy from the Harvard Business School where we talked about *people* being a company's greatest asset. So, I decided to focus my work on people, not just as a company's greatest asset, but the greatest asset we have as a global society. The connection of people is what will save us from falling into the great abyss of loneliness, disconnect, and the utter demise of happiness, care and compassion for one another. Our humanity is the very thing that will continue to bring us hope for a better and more connected tomorrow. All of that time and research I have been doing throughout my career adds up to tell us one very important story.

The majority of those who lead others feel like they are constrained by the very organization they are working to build and grow. In the age of digital transformation, one of the most important things a leader can do is to remember the needs of their people. This "transformation" needs to be about the human as much as it is about the technology. In addition, the striving and growth goal is really in the ability to do both and to become what we have decided to call, based on our own proprietary research, a **"Relational Leader."**

In finding ways to harness our Human Leadership behaviors, we will be able to harness human potential for peak performance. This book aims to bridge the gap between personal or leadership development and peak performance by providing a comprehensive guide to fostering an environment where every team member not only feels valued but is also empowered to contribute their best. The scope extends beyond traditional leadership tactics to explore how these core principles and behaviors can be intricately woven into daily leadership practices.

These past five years have been like nothing we have ever known before. And yet, somehow, we have managed our way through. Sometimes in ugly tears, and fear, and pain. Yet, still we arrived here. Together. Heart-centered, full-intentioned, and curious enough to know how the story continues ... and ... how it ends.

Each of us has a story to tell. Each of us is a part of the grander story to which we collectively add as we allow or are given the space to do so. I don't have a crystal ball and I bet a good majority of us truly have no idea what comes next. The fact remains: you own the pen and you can write it however you want. How you choose to live out this next chapter becomes your legacy.

In that choice, I hope this book will help lay out a model for a collective movement forward: a kind of "what now" guide to help you find ways to fully exhale and find the calm and connection we all seek. And most importantly, to find a new way to build connections with the communities around us. It is in this complex landscape that I introduce a transformative approach through the lens of ***B.R.A.V.E.*** Human Leadership behaviors—**B**elonging, **R**esilience, **A**uthenticity, **V**ulnerability, and **E**mpathy.

I purposefully wrote this book in three different parts. Part One serves as a collection of stories that bring forward the real ways these concepts live and breathe. In modeling these behaviors, it is my hope, to build a relationship, trust, and a connection with you prior to laying the foundation for the explanation of B.R.A.V.E. Part Two will focus on the concepts of B.R.A.V.E. Human Leadership itself. In this part, you will understand how the five B.R.A.V.E. pillars are critical to each way in which we connect with others, from the ability to create cultures of belonging around us everywhere we show up, to leaning into empathy in our everyday conversations. Finally, Part Three will take us into the age of digital transformation and the importance of human skills above all else to understand what lies ahead. Through the lens of five different former professional and Olympic level athletes, Part Three will also help us to understand what we call "Relational Leadership" and why it is the style of leadership that has the best opportunity for success today as it is the measurement of highest performance AND highest people skills.

What this book means to you and how you use it is for you to determine. The moment you held this book in your hands, it became "OUR journey." As we are writing "OUR B.R.A.V.E. story" together, I hope and pray you will never feel alone on this path ahead and that you know, deep down inside, you are more than enough. Sometimes we just need a reminder of that. Let this serve as yours. I created the B.R.A.V.E. Human Leadership model to be just that: a reminder and a guide to take us from where we are to what has the promise of being better days ahead in business and beyond. Whether in the boardroom, the classroom, the living room, or the locker room, we can find ways to do it better. Connected Cultures and Relational Leaders aren't just NICE to have, they are a NEED to have, and we need them today more than ever. We need to find new ways to create safe spaces where belonging is the central intention.

I set out to explore how we connect to each other and how certain behaviors that we lack (or think we lack) seem to hold us back from getting what we want or from living the lives we have always dreamed. No, it's not easy. I am not going to tell you that it is. I won't wave a magic wand and make all of the hard go away. With resilience, we find we are so much stronger than we think we are.

I was inspired to write this book after witnessing numerous talented leaders struggle with balancing the human aspect of leadership with their performance objectives. Their challenges often echoed in our conversations: how to be approachable yet assertive, compassionate yet strong, understanding yet uncompromising on quality and customer experience. Each story shared a common theme: a desire to lead with empathy and authenticity without sacrificing results. These experiences underscored the need for a new paradigm in leadership: one that equips leaders with the tools to harness the full potential of their teams through genuine connection and understanding. Leaders like you, who are deeply invested in both the welfare and performance of your teams, will find this book a beacon guiding you towards more holistic and effective leadership strategies.

The foundations laid out in these pages are built upon cutting-edge research in psychology and neuroscience, alongside timeless wisdom from renowned leaders and thinkers who have been doing this work and have laid this path. I am grateful for the insights and contributions from various experts whose perspectives have enriched this narrative. This book is for those of you who aspire to master the delicate balance of leading with heart and mind.

To each of you who has chosen to embark on this journey by picking up this book, I thank you. Your commitment to evolving as a leader is commendable, and I am confident that the insights contained here will support you in creating not just a more productive, but also a more empathetic team environment. By integrating these behaviors into your leadership style, you can expect transformative results, enhanced team dynamics, a nurturing yet high-performing culture, and, most importantly, a greater sense of fulfillment in your role as a leader.

I know there is no way I would have been able to do this without some really amazing and important people in my circle. Accordingly, I have an unbound gratitude I wish to express.

Please bear with me as I do just that:

*Thank you ...*

*To my Mom and Dad who taught me so much and modeled for me what it means to have a servant heart and authenticity and love for humanity. For the guidance, love, and support that helped me hang on even in the darkest of times. On this earth or the next time and space, you are a part of my soul forever.*

*To my family and friends for your love and uplifting spirit that has woven a steady thread throughout my life. I am forever grateful for all of it. Every time, place, and way you have shown up, I admire your capacity for love and your ability to SEE me in all my flaws and all my realness with grace and compassion. I owe you the world and all the love in it.*

*To my team ... When I say I couldn't do this without you it isn't a pleasantry. I mean it. I would NOT be able to do this without you. Every laugh, every tear, every heart-centered conversation just makes us all better. I know for sure I have found the right people to help me put this work out into the world. You keep my world spinning, and, somehow, at the same time keep me from falling off as it continues to move faster. Eileen, Michelle, Cristina: my sincere gratitude for shouldering that burden.*

*To my coaches and mentors, especially David Newman and Danielle LaPorte: My gratitude for always reminding me of who I am and, in the moments I forget, reminding me of the power I hold in my own hands.*

*To my wife, JJ. You are my muse and my best friend. You are not just my love and life partner, but my laugh partner. Thank you for the inspiration you provide me, the unwavering support you afford me, and the unconditional love you pour into me on a daily* basis. You are my very best "yes" and I wouldn't want to do life with anyone else. You are my rock. I am grateful for our every day adventures and for the joy and love in our daily EBC journey, no matter the outcome.

To Benson, Quinley, and Piper, our beautiful fur-baby labs. Thank you for reminding me every day what unconditional love looks like. I often say I don't know what we did as humans to deserve dogs, but I know for sure that life is so much better with them to make us laugh, to cuddle with and play fetch with in the middle of the workday.

Lastly, thank YOU for coming along on this ride with me and being my reason for the work I do. These last 15-plus years have led me to this place and time. It has been the journey of a lifetime. There is no question, the best is yet to come.

*I will meet you there.*
*JLC*

# CHAPTER 1

## How did we get here?

The sound of gravel under the tires of our 1974 wood-paneled, green, Ford Country Squire station wagon made my eyes pop open abruptly. I was so confused. I swear I had just fallen asleep. Still trying to open my eyes fully, I felt the sudden pain in the back of my upper right thigh and hip. I shifted quickly so the seat belt connector that was rigidly sticking up from that hard, front, middle seat would stop poking me.

The air was cold and almost like a wind tunnel as my parents had both the front doors wide open, as they pulled the things out that were shoved under the seats to make space for all 7 of us and all of our stuff. One of which, I am sure, was my coat. I was always hot in the car and still, to this day, can't sit in a car with a coat on. I always remember the hundreds of times my mom would yell at my dad if he turned the heat up through the vents. She hated hot air blowing in her face. As do I.

"We're here!" my dad shouted through a yawn and a vocally loud stretch as my mom was fumbling with my coat, trying to get it on my dead weight five-year-old body, not even out of the car yet. The others had already made their way to the door. I was still fighting the seatbelt and the coat, not sure of where we were and if we were just getting home, arriving at the place we may have been heading, or if I even remembered where that was in the first place.

The many hours spent falling asleep in that front, hard, middle seat with those double-no-give- seat belt connectors is such a clear memory from my childhood. Visiting relatives, vacations in the mountains, wherever we went, I would wake up to the sound of arriving. The same thought came to mind each time, "How did we get here?" I would begin to open my eyes as I shifted in my seat, put my coat back on, and, with eyes half closed, climbed down out of the car and into whatever adventure we had embarked upon, even if it was just coming home.

I have asked this question "How did we get here?" when in the middle of a sticky situation, when with the softball teams I coached who were down a couple runs late in the game, or when I wasn't paying attention to the process. I have found it is extremely difficult to know the answer if we were asleep for most of the ride on the way to where we are.

This journey we all have been on. This shared experience of the past few years, feels for some of us like we are in that uncomfortable front middle seat. Not knowing where we were going before we woke up to the arriving. Here, in this place we have never been, the cold drafty air hitting our tired selves as we try unsuccessfully to put our coats on, that one sleeve we can never seem to find behind our backs, as we make our way out of the car and into the here and now … wherever that may be.

We have been living in a time of racial unrest and of heated political divide leading to anger and hatred. We have seen war-devastated countries in our midst and people struggling just to exist. We have watched as a global pandemic ravaged our whole world, our heroes in healthcare, first responders, teachers, and all other front-line essential workers, who are burned out and asked again every single day to find more to give from the bottom of an empty well. We have watched as wars rage on still, in places we may have never been, and in those that we may call home. It all feels so heavy. I can't help but ask loudly, "**How did we get here?!**"

We have never done all of this at once before. And yet, every day that we are still on this side of the ground, we continue to do it. We seem to find a way to figure it out even when it's been hard. And it has been hard.

I don't know if we will ever know the answer to "How did we get *here*?" However, I *do* know that we can take some time collectively to figure out where we go from here. *We* didn't ask for these challenges to hit us all at once. We never do. We didn't have any idea what was about to happen when we rang in the new year on January 1, 2020. And yet, the truth is, - we *never* do.

What makes this different now is that we can intentionally make choices to take the next right step toward writing a better story and moving in a new direction from here. Beyond the hurt, grief, and loss is healing, compassion, and grace for us all. Between here and there, the questions remain:

> **What story are we telling?**
> **What legacy are we leaving?**

Let's face it, what we were doing wasn't working. This idea that we could work ourselves to burnout, overcommit and underdeliver, and try not to lose ourselves in the process wasn't realistic. It has never shown itself to be sustainable. We have found ways to make ourselves more stressed, more sick, more unhappy, and more unwell. Just to have … more?

The gift we are given right now is the daily reminder to shift our weight off of the seat belt buckle. It's in the intentional moments we get to have with our families and being present in the moments we may have been too hurried to have before. Taking a moment to take it all in. The day, the people around us, the sun and even just a good deep breath.

For those who learned how to work from home in a dress shirt and a pair of ratty old sweatpants in the midst of the pandemic, to have a midday break to walk with the dogs, no commute, no traffic, no heels or suits. For some even now, it looks so different today than even just a few years ago, moments we didn't ask for and yet perhaps can find some goodness in.

> *"We get to choose how we respond in the midst of what is hard and how we show up in community and connection with one another."*
>
> *-jlc*

We get a choice now. Maybe not in how we got here, but in what's next. We get to choose how we respond in the midst of what is hard and how we show up in community and connection with each other going forward.

I was 11 when my family bought our vacation home in the Pocono Mountains that we called "The Ark." Of course, my Dad named it after a biblical reference. It was a place we could all safely gather to reconnect and be together. We hosted annual family reunions with upwards of 60-70 people. We played games into the wee hours of the night. We watched scary movies on VHS tapes that we rented from the one video store within a 45-mile radius. We laughed and had some great and not-so-great times there. We cried and fought and watched for shooting stars and went to county fairs.

The month before my thirteenth birthday, this time in the backseat next to my mom as my brother drove, we hurried down the windy mountain roads to the hospital that was a good 45 minutes away to meet a cardiologist. My Dad was having chest pains as we were about to go to the basement for a family game of ping pong. He sat in the front seat to direct my brother who had just gotten his learner's permit and who, I'm pretty certain, was not supposed to be driving at night. As we turned a corner, he slammed on the breaks, making my dad brace himself on the dashboard. My mom threw her proverbial "mom arm" across my shoulders so I didn't go flying into the front seat. I strained my eyes in the pitch black to see past my brother's seat and into that middle spot I used to claim as my own to see why he would stop like that.

As my eyes focused in the dark, I saw a big head with a very large eye looking right back at us. It was a cow. **In the middle of the road.** If my dad wasn't having a heart attack prior to this, he certainly had to be having one now, I thought.

We finally arrived at the hospital safely to find out my dad would be admitted and needed an angiogram. A few days later we were informed he had a mild heart attack and would need an angioplasty. We went home to New Jersey and a few weeks later, on my mom's 50th birthday, he would have open heart surgery in New York City at the Cornell Medical Center. He was 48 years old.

As I write this, I am having a moment of realization since my big milestone birthday last year, that I am currently the same age as my Mom when Dad had his surgery. So the question begs to be asked again: How *did* we get here?

Moments and memories I won't ever have again, some I couldn't even recall if I needed to. Whole chunks of time that I couldn't even tell you how they were spent; they just happened. And now, they are gone.

Those times I was on autopilot, not knowing where I was going, but waking up to the sound of arriving. And maybe sometimes waking up to the sound of leaving, jobs, relationships, mistakes, and regret. Whatever the thing, we are either coming into a problem, coming out of a problem, or we're in the midst of a problem now. Our humanness is predicated on how awake we are in the moment and how much we can tolerate in the waking.

We are creatures of habit. We move our hand away from the flame for the most part, but only when it gets too hot. Too often, we don't actually make the connection to not put our hand IN the flame to begin with. "How DID we get here?" is exactly like that. Figuring out what would make us STOP wanting to touch the fire that we KNOW will burn us may or may not change the outcome. Asking how we got here is often useless in that regard as it doesn't really fix the issue or tell us what caused the issue in the first place. We are here. It doesn't matter if we took a plane or a train or a car or a boat. Does it? Or … does it …? Will asking how we got here make us not get here again? Or since we already know the way, maybe it doesn't make it harder, but actually easier to find it the next time? Do we ask anyway … for the sake of asking? To try hard to do it differently now? To do it better?

Regardless of the hard questions the truth remains: We have arrived. We are awake. We know now that we are here in the midst of the searching. What that next right step is will be up to us, and how we figure it out is probably what will change the course of all that is yet to come. In taking a collective deep breath, and waiting for each other to be ready to exhale, we can dig up a different kind of energy that most won't ever know in their lifetime. We are the lucky ones. We GET to be alive right now and we GET to know that we have a choice to either be in the way or become the way. We can be the match or we can be the bucket of water. Knowing which is needed at the right time is always the key.

As we navigate this, knowing we need to recognize and embrace the importance of discomfort, WE WILL be uncomfortable at times. That is where real growth lies: outside the comfort of what we know to be true. Maybe instead of the front hard middle seat or even the back seat where we have no control, we climb into the driver's seat and take the wheel. We make it known who we are and what we want from this one beautiful life we hold in our very own hands. We make a choice. A loud and decisive choice. And as we do, we unapologetically wake up to the sound of our very own arriving. This time knowing where we are and why we are here and, most of all, knowing where we want to go next. This knowledge will undoubtedly lead us forward. And the only way forward is to recognize that it is truly our humanity at the core that matters; that it is connection and community that undoubtedly will save us.

The road ahead is up to us.
The truth is it always has been.
The pen is yours.
Write what you want the next chapter to say.
Shift to a comfortable spot.
Get your coat on if you want.
Together, we exhale.
And it is only together that I am ready to arrive at this next beautiful adventure.
Buckle up.
We ride at dawn.

# CHAPTER 2

# Connection in a Disconnected World

> *"I define connection as the energy that exists between people when they feel seen, heard and valued; when they can give and receive without judgment; and when they derive sustenance and strength from the relationship."*[1]
> —*Brené Brown.*

It's about a three-hour drive from Downingtown to Williamsport, Pennsylvania at 5:30 in the morning. I needed to be there by 8:30 so the "corporate CEOs" could interview me for their big moment on stage introducing me to the 400+ audience. The interesting part of these "CEOs" is that they were all juniors and seniors …. in high school.

Every first week in August for about seven years, I made that drive up to Lycoming College to speak at the annual Pennsylvania Free Enterprise Week (PFEW) camp. It was truly one of my favorite events each year and I loved spending this time with these incredible humans who dedicate their lives to helping young adults reach their full potential. I have spoken at places like Samsung, Nike, the NIH , the US Department of Defense, and Procter & Gamble and I get paid very well to do so. Yet this event, which I do not do for the money, has been so special and so important to me. I feel like I get to give back and help our younger generation develop the confidence to stand tall and find their voice. For some, that may be the most important lesson of their high school career, maybe even their whole lives.

A few years ago, I was nearing the end of the line of students who came up to say hi to me after my presentation. Some wanted pictures, others just wanted to say thank you and shake my hand. Some had really smart questions and some wanted to share something they connected with or tell me they lived in my town and asked if I knew their parents. That always gave me a good chuckle and on the off chance that I did, it's always nice to meet a friend's child who I may not have met otherwise. They often will give me the inside scoop on "said friend" and let me know how they REALLY are at home. Just kidding friends, they keep your secrets. I promise.

There were three students left in line and as I was nearing the end and getting ready to pack up and make the drive back down the mountain, the last girl quietly walked up to me. Her head was down. I couldn't see her eyes, but tears were bouncing across the tops of her torn blue Converse high tops. As she slowly lifted her head, we made eye contact.

"Hi," she choked out in a whisper, "I'm Annie." She was looking right at me now, her blue eyes piercing and still wet from the last tear that just escaped down her cheek and onto her shoe.

"Hi Annie," I smiled at her as warmly as I could, wanting to know her story. A thousand moments of this exact feeling ran through my head. The sadness, the lost surrender, the ache. It all came rushing back. Too familiar, and full of my own discomfort. I quickly kept talking, "It's really great to meet you. I am so glad you showed up with me today."

Her lips slowly morphed into the beginnings of a smile. She responded slowly, her voice shaking, "I just wanted to say thank you. This is the first time in my life I have ever felt seen."

Without a word, I reached out my arms and gave her a hug. It was instinct. "*Oh love, I see you. I really see you and you are so so important to this world,*" I screamed to myself inside my own head. I know these words. I know these feelings. I so often wanted to hear those words for myself (not that I never got them growing up). I think it was more of a self-imposed isolation that I created. I didn't share my inner thoughts or fears or secrets. Sometimes I think by not wanting to let anyone in, I created the loneliness I often wanted to try to run away from, not really knowing I held the power to my own connection.

I am an extroverted introvert who has felt unseen for a large part of my life. I can recognize now that some of it was due to my own assumptions and, therefore, partially my own doing. Other parts of it was being the youngest of five, much-older-than-me siblings, all off living their own lives before I even got to middle school. Either way, I have sat in this place before. And it wasn't a great place to hang out.

I finally said something after the hug ended, "I do see you. I AM you."

And then quickly, she was gone. As I watched her walk away, with her head just slightly higher than she arrived, I caught the tear as it jumped off my face and before it could hit my own laces. It fills me with a sense of purpose knowing that I can affect a life wherever I go. I did my job that day and, maybe even more so, Annie ended up affecting mine. I spent the drive home realizing how important this work is. These conversations aren't only critical, but they can be life-changing and … <u>life-saving</u>.

About the same time that COVID-19 required us to distance ourselves from each other, move meetings to screens of isolation, and family gatherings to Zoom rooms, I had a conversation with a client named Tom. He shared a simple story with me about something that he was feeling deeply.

One night in mid-2020, in the dim glow of his laptop, Tom sat hunched over the kitchen table; the quiet hum of the refrigerator–his only companion in the otherwise silent apartment. The digital clock ticked past midnight, casting a soft, blue light that mingled with the shadows. He scrolled through his social media feed, a mosaic of smiling faces and curated lives passing by under his fingertips. Each click, each swipe deepened his sense of isolation.

Tom paused on a photo of old college friends gathered at a recent reunion he had missed. Their laughter seemed to echo through the digital silence that enveloped him. He remembered their last meeting. Conversations that were once deep and engaging had been reduced to brief exchanges and superficial chatter. The screen's glow did little to warm the growing chill he felt inside.

Outside, a dog barked sharply, breaking Tom's reverie. He glanced through the window where a gentle rain began to tap against the glass, blurring the streetlights into halos of amber light. The city breathed around him, alive and distant. Turning back to his laptop, he wondered about the authenticity lost in these digital exchanges. How could one forge real connections when interactions felt so … on the surface?

He recalled a recent video call with his sister. She had tried to express her frustrations about work, but frequent interruptions and poor connection had left them both feeling more separated than before. Tom sighed and closed his laptop with a soft snap. He missed the nuances of face-to-face conversations: the shared silences, understanding smiles, and comforting gestures.

With a stretch and a yawn, he decided it was time for bed. As he brushed his teeth, staring at his reflection in the foggy mirror, he contemplated how different it was to see himself here than how others saw him online: filtered and framed into what he thought they wanted to see.

Climbing into bed, Tom lay awake listening to the rhythm of the rain on the rooftop. His mind wandered through memories of deeper connections now faded into acquaintances due to neglect or distance imposed by life's relentless march or perhaps by reliance on digital communication's convenience.

He paused after retelling the story and asked the question that has stayed with me since:

**"Are We Truly Connected or Merely Interacting?"**

We are the most technologically connected society ever, yet we stand in the midst of being the most disconnected and isolated at the same time. Why is that? How did we get *here*? It often feels as if we are living in the age of digital hearts, of not knowing where the bliss of a new technology actually joins with the emotion of all that's human. The moments that are real and tangible and yet so disconnected they are hard to actually hold onto. And yet, I believe we *can* have both. We just need to master letting go of the fear that holds us back from all of it.

Understanding this also requires some willingness to take ownership and accountability for how we are showing up in the world every day. Are we spending our free hour or two between tucking the kids in and climbing into bed scrolling and swiping? Are we walking the dog in the morning before we head to work, whether in the office or virtually, watching TikTok videos and Instagram reels, comparing our lives with those of others we see through a screen?

I took some time recently to check in with myself about this. I recognized that perhaps I was spending too much time doing that too. Although there is nothing wrong with spending some time on social media to connect, I realized I was allowing myself to get lost in things that didn't serve me, and that my yearning to connect was actually disconnecting me from real life too often.

The time we spend living vicariously through others' "posted" lives could be time we spend living our own. I am a work in progress with that. I sense I always will be. I question how much of that vicariously living in the "elsewhere" is just a purposeful distraction from living in the "here," which, for so many, can often be brutal. Are we craving connection so much that it feels like we can, at least, however distantly or one-sidedly, be in each other's lives when we are Facebook Friends or Instagram Followers, connecting in name only? I have often met someone who said, "I feel like I know you already; I follow you on social media." While we do crave connection, I often wonder if we are actually getting to the level of connection that we truly desire. The link between connection and loneliness has been studied and written about for years. The findings mostly center on how we all feel better mentally, emotionally, and even physically when we are in relationships with others. In a 2015 study done by Martino, Pegg, and Frates, published in the *American Journal of Lifestyle Medicine*, the findings were quite clear: when the participants had regular connection with others, they showed higher cancer survival rates, lower blood sugars, a decrease in cardiovascular death, and mitigation of posttraumatic stress disorder symptoms.[2] It is undeniably clear that we are born with a need for connection.

> *"Incorporating social support and connections is critical for overall health and for healthy habits to be sustainable".[3]*

The research shows that there is evidence of human beings living in groups for thousands of years. In fact, Holt-Lundstad and colleagues at Brigham Young University investigated 148 published articles that were focused on the effects of social connection with friends, family, coworkers, and neighbors.[4] The results of their study supported an increased survival rate of 50% for cardiovascular disease. This happens to also be the highest odds of survival compared to other well associated mitigating risk factors across the board.[5] **Bottom line**: The link between human connection and good health has now been, without a doubt, well established.[6]

In her book, *The Village Effect*, psychologist and author Susan Pinker writes about her discovery of a small mountain village on the island of Sardinia. The people of the village put a lot of stock into face-to-face conversation and connection and would spend time daily doing so.[7] Interestingly (and seemingly not by coincidence), they also happen to have one of the highest life expectancies in the world.[7] As far as I can tell, connection is deeply entwined with the state of our mental health. The experts have connected the dots pretty easily. Even the National Alliance on Mental Illnesses created a campaign called "You Are Not Alone." When we remind each other that we are all connected in some way, it makes us just feel better. How often have you heard someone say, "just knowing someone else is there makes me not feel so alone?" In fact, Mental Health America found that 71% of people they surveyed turned to friends and family in times of stress.[8] We CRAVE connection. It's how we operate as human beings.

The paralysis of anxiety and depression is no stranger to my body. It's hard to find the energy or desire do ANYTHING when we feel isolated and alone. It's kind of like we hit the off switch and our light dims or just completely goes out. If you know that feeling, it's one of despair and insurmountable struggle. So often, just a simple reboot, reconnection, or boost of kindness and compassion can get things moving again. All of us want to be seen and listened to, as this validates our human experience. This requires real connections to others.

It was 1996, and I had just graduated the year before from the University of Delaware (UD) with my Bachelor's in English and a concentration in Journalism. I was going to be the next Barbara Walters. (In case you wondered, I'm actually not her and only a wee bit younger.) I remember sitting at my table in my dining/kitchen area of my apartment that I moved into right out of college, trying to get the floppy disk to go into the slot of my Apple Macintosh II. It wasn't working. It was my first computer, and the dial-up sounds were extra loud. Except this time it wasn't doing anything. The screen was blank.

I was still a newbie. We just started having computer labs at the end of my four years at UD, and using them was always a little overwhelming. Not to mention the fact that I could NEVER remember the email address the school gave me that was three lines long and had music composers' names in the middle. I still never figured out why that was.

Despite my best efforts, it was getting late. The screen was still dark and the disk still wouldn't slide in. It was over an hour since I flipped the switch on and 6:30am would come quickly. I couldn't stay up and figure out how not to die of dysentery playing the video game "Oregon Trail" anyway, it was time to get some sleep. I left it for the next day.

After work, I made the seven-minute drive home as fast as I could, threw my jacket on the rocking chair next to the sliding glass door and sat in the old, wooden chair in the dining room. It creaked every time I moved it away from the table to settle in. There was a number the IT guy gave me at work. He said to call this guy Steve and see if he could help. He worked for some technology company help desk. Not really knowing what that all meant, I found the crumpled ripped piece of paper in my pocket and dialed the number.

"Hello IT, can I help you?"

"Uhh. Yeah, I hope so," I said slowly. Where and who is this guy and how much will this cost me? I panicked for a moment and then snapped my attention back to the call.

"OK? What kind of machine are you calling about?"

"Well, how do I know that? There is an apple on it. And a roman numeral two. Does that help?"

With a slight chuckle of both annoyance and probably thinking I was a pathetic, helpless caller who doesn't know my head from my ass, he answered. "Umm, yeah. OK. So what's the problem?"

"Well," I quickly tried to get my thoughts together to make some kind of sense about something I didn't understand. "I tried to put the floppy disk in." I paused. Shit. That's what it's called right? Now he is REALLY going to think I am stupid.

"Yeah, ok … … and …..?"

*Yeah, he was definitely getting annoyed.* I continued quickly, "Uhh …It won't go in."

This was well before the time of "that's what she said jokes," but I think I probably snickered anyway. "Actually, it won't do anything." I was silently waiting for him to tell me what to do next.

"Ma'am?" I couldn't tell if he wanted a response but now by his silence after what was definitely a question, I jumped in.

"Yes?" Ok, here it comes. He is going to tell me what to do to magically make it work and I am going to fix a computer. I felt kind of powerful for a moment until his voice began again.

"Is it … plugged in?"

My first reaction was one of irritation. I mean, that's a stupid question. Is it plugged in?! DUH …. "Of course it's …"

He could tell by my silence that perhaps we had stumbled upon the grand prize. I thought it was going to be a very difficult string of characters he wanted me to type to program some kind of something where the screen goes black and the white blinking letters and symbols make the thing run … something called "DOS" or something of the sort. But no. It wasn't at all that.

The stupid thing wasn't plugged in. "Well, shit," I replied as I dropped my head, shaking it slowly back and forth in shame and frustration.

I laughed audibly now. And after a few seconds of deafening silence, his booming laughter shook the phone receiver against my ear the same way the ring of my phone reverberated off the walls of the moving truck in 2012.

"You'd be surprised ma'am. This happens every day."

Simple. THIS HAPPENS EVERY DAY.

How did I expect for anything to work when it wasn't even plugged in?

This is what connection is all about. Finding ways to stay plugged in, even when we struggle to do so, even if it looks different than what we imagined or are used to. Even when we are still trying to figure it out. Even when we don't know how.

Here we are in the age of global pandemics, racial unrest, and war: a time of division and isolation not before felt in my lifetime. Prior to COVID-19, we were told that we need to stay socially connected. All of that changed beginning on a Friday afternoon in March 2020. We had been asked to isolate ourselves for the better part of two years and to keep our distance even from family. We were asked to use virtual meetings instead of face-to-face, and if we could see loved ones on video instead of in person, we should do that instead. What we have learned about the importance of in-person connection as a positive impact on longevity was all of a sudden something that could kill us too. What a twist of fate.

As the world has settled into what seems to be a feasible long-term hybrid approach to work, strategies to infuse digital conversations with intention and authenticity involve more than just choosing the right words. They require an understanding of the emotional undertones and a deliberate effort to convey our true selves. Active listening and showing vulnerability play pivotal roles in bridging emotional distances. By being present in our interactions and expressing genuine interest in others' experiences and feelings, we pave the way for deeper connections.

As we will discover, vulnerability in our digital communications can transform ordinary interactions into opportunities for meaningful engagement. Sharing our struggles and uncertainties can encourage others to open up, creating a space where authentic relationships can flourish despite physical distances. We are searching for connection in a disconnected world. Whether in person or digitally, finding our way back together is our next right thing.

When we look back in history, through all the "stuff" the past four years has thrown at us, we will find that we have always been right here, together. We are all entwined, through every group we associate with, every office we enter into, every family we play soccer with, every congregation we worship with, or every crowd we sing with during the seventh-inning stretch. This connection isn't something that a deep divide, social unrest, or global pandemic can tear apart. It is deeper than that. On a human level, we belong to each other. In that belonging, we find our way home.

Even on the hardest of days and the darkest of nights, know you will always be able to find your own power cord. Unplug when you need to, just don't spend too much time there. When you're ready, sit back and take a deep breath.

Go ahead now and plug in.

We've been waiting for you.

## CHAPTER 3

# Be Where Your Feet Are

I moved to Tenafly, NJ when I was seven. I was lucky enough to have a boy and a girl, named James and Alysia, next door to play with who were both around my age. We quickly became close friends and Alysia and I ended up being inseparable. If I wanted to play and Alysia wasn't home, James would come over with his box of baseball cards and I would meet him outside with mine. We would meet at the pitcher's mound. Usually, I would bring a stick I would find on my walk out the back door to our small makeshift "field" in my backyard. After picking our teams out of our baseball cards, doing some trades, and picking who would go first, our World Series would begin.

If we hit the wiffle ball far enough over each other's heads, we could typically get from the crabapple tree to the big maple in the middle of the yard, around to the side of the garage. That was third base. We would then put the baseball card of the player who "hit it" on the base we got to and go back to pick up the bat to swing again for the next batter. We would play from the time we got up and ate breakfast until it got too dark to see the ball at all. In the summer, we often kept score and went back out the next day to continue our best-of-seven series.

It was clear even before we moved there that I had a deep love and infatuation with baseball. I knew every player's uniform number, what team he played on, what position he played, and often, even where he hit in the lineup. When I was five, I would sit on my great-grandmother's veranda and listen to the Phillies on the radio …for the ENTIRE GAME. My parents were always amazed that I could sit still for that long. It was the one thing that could always lock me in. I am more amazed that I was a Phillies fan back then, but Grandma Palmer wouldn't have it any other way. GO Yanks!

In Late March of 1981, we walked into the darkly lit wood paneled room in the municipal building in the middle of town. It smelled musty, somewhat like Grandma's basement. We walked right up to the table labeled "Registration A-M", Dad leading the way. I don't really remember whose idea it was to go, if I made it clear I wanted to play or if my parents were just trying to find ways for me to run around to burn off the "extra energy." It could have been since it was the first spring in our new town, if it was really about meeting more kids. Being that my very first day of school was my birthday, bringing brownies to kindergarten in my lobster red sundress was a sure way to make instant friends. My parents seemed to own the corner on that plan. Clearly, making friends was high on the agenda. Perhaps they were ahead of the curve and knew just how important social connections would be. We'll never know.

I recall some fear as we walked into the municipal building, but I kept quiet. In my quick glance around the room full of dads and maybe two moms, I saw little boys everywhere. Some I recognized from my school and some I didn't know at all. There was a pretty good probability that since there were four elementary schools in town, I would know only a quarter of the eager ballplayers in the room. I still hid behind Dad's legs with my head down hoping none of that quarter would see and recognize me. I looked around again. The realization that I was the *only* girl in the room had started to sink in. And yet not really knowing what that would mean, I nodded and smiled at the older man behind the clipboard on the other side of the table. Quickly, after my Dad asked about payment and when the league started, we walked out. On our way back to the car in the brisk night breeze, he unlocked my door with a quiet glance and then hurried to his side of the brown Oldsmobile Cutlass Supreme Brougham. He got in and shut the door.

"Ok, so you are all signed up for Little League Baseball, Sweets." Sweets. It was the name he had called me since I was born, and I looked at him fiercely as soon as it left his mouth. I frowned, I'm sure.

"Maybe don't call me that when the boys are around Daddy."

He smiled and quickly tried to make a serious face that always came with one of his eyebrows twitching so we knew he wasn't serious at all. "Ok, Sweets. I won't"

I stared out the window for the whole 6-minute drive home.

Those first few years, I was the only girl on the team and I also happened to bat cleanup and made the all star game each year. In my second year playing, I have no idea why or when I decided I wanted to be the catcher, but I told my Dad I wanted to go behind the plate. At this point, Dad was clearly enamored by the need to control 20-some little uniforms haplessly swinging bats, hoping not to hit each other and forgetting helmets or gloves each week. By this time, he was the coach, but he was still also my Dad. So, I remember when I was just able to remember things, he told me I could be or do anything I worked hard to be ... or do. I called a serious meeting and told him I wanted to be the catcher. After some back and forth, and my Mom saying no for fear I would get hurt, my Dad finally agreed. It was either the dimple, the blue eyes, or the pouty lip–I am not exactly sure which one did it that time, but it worked. If I worked on it in the backyard and I could catch the best pitcher at the next practice, he would put me in a game … if Mom agreed. The excitement in my blue eyes was for sure what always got her. She paused for a few moments before responding. Finally, she said yes.

If you are reading this and know me, you know how that went. When I get something in my head that I want to do or accomplish, I don't stop until I have it in my grasp or at least tried whole-heartedly until it is sure not to happen. After breakfast, and until the sun went down, I put the gear on that weekend, knowing practice was the next day, and threw rubber pinky balls off the garage door to practice catching them with that crazy big catcher's mitt. I was no stranger to making the backyard my stadium. This time alone, I did it until my knees were tired and sore, the old rickety yellow light on the garage flickered in the darkness, and dinner was getting cold.

One of the exercises we would do to practice blocking as a catcher was to replace your feet with your knees. We'd drop down quickly but come down directly on our knees in the same spot our feet were so we didn't move out or sideways. Thank God for leg and knee guards because that was brutal and I completely understand why I have knee issues today. What that concept also reminds me of beyond the physical time and space is to stay in the moment emotionally and mentally as well. When we are present, we change the whole scene, the whole picture, and it becomes impossible to be in two places at once. Feet. Knees. Feet. Knees. Nowhere else but here. Watching the great catchers of my time, it was always that. Be where your feet are. I wanted to be great like that too.

That next game, the starting catcher happened to be sick and called to tell my Dad he wasn't able to play. On the ride over to Sunnyside Park, the clouds and drizzle making their irony known, my Dad said he had to mess with the lineup because we had a few kids who couldn't make it.

"Howard's brother was getting Bar Mitzvah'd, Jimmy was sick, and Josh's cousins are in town."

I quickly snapped my head from watching the wipers lull me with their slow cadence, to my dad's profile, his goatee looking greyer than yesterday.

"Wait. Jimmy is sick?" I tried not to sound happy about that, because really, in my heart I would usually be sad that he was sick and would miss a game. I know I never wanted to miss a game.

I sat quietly for a minute. "So … who is going to catch?"

I was still, waiting fairly impatiently for his answer.

He reached behind the seat to the clipboard he threw in as we were hurrying to not be late to the field and put it on my lap. On the game book was the lineup written in his very distinct left-handed scribble. I searched for my name. There I was. Third in the order today. Hmmm … I wondered why that was. I quickly forgot about the order when I saw the pointy letter C and the rest of the oddly connected letters … CATCH.

Catch. Usually, he abbreviated out of pure time constraints. Today, it was in all caps. *Me? I am catching?? Really?* I did a total 90 degree turn in the seat, the seatbelt almost ripping my ear off.

"Can you handle it?" he said in that dad tone that is half question, half "I have confidence in you so don't screw it up" way.

"Yes. I am the catcher. I will do it good."

Exactly the words my Mom echoed from upstairs over the vacuum cleaner before we left.

"Do it good!" was her way of reminding me that I was enough. Somehow three short words empowered me to know "I could" no matter what it was. She said that before every test I took in school, every game I played, and even before the speech I gave running for treasurer in the fourth grade. It was her quick and simple pump-up reminder and her way of cheering me on. It was also her way of telling me she loved me. I did happen to lose that fourth-grade election, however. Even if my "put your lucky penny down on Jenny" poster captured the best slogan in town. Regardless, Mom and Dad had a knack for keeping me grounded in the present moment.

Just as we pulled into the field parking lot, I was out of the car before it actually came to a stop, got my cleats on, and was waiting for my Dad to hurry up and turn off the engine. We walked through the mist that was now starting to clear and onto the far field in the opposite corner of the park. My dad was carrying the oddly shaped equipment bag that always looked like we had snatched a body from somewhere along the way.

A quick warmup and into the gear I went. First, the shin guards. The clasps were getting old and I often had knot the straps so they were hard to get on and off. Then, the chest protector that always felt like I was wearing an oversized bib. Lastly, the helmet which back then consisted of a batting helmet or sometimes a cap backwards and a mask that slid tightly over top and pressed my chin in so hard I that my jaw ached all night after wearing it for more than an hour.

None of that mattered now. I was the catcher. As I was taught, the catcher was in charge.

*Meet Them Where They Are*

I was the only one who could look out and see the whole field at once. I was kind of like a football quarterback, but behind home plate. This was my team and it was my job to be a vocal leader and tell them what was happening at any moment when they couldn't see from their position.

My Dad met at home plate with the umpire and other coach to go over rules and flip the coin to see who would be the home team. As they shook hands, I was standing right next to the field by the backstop, waiting. Like a suitcase that is stuffed too full and about to burst, I could hardly keep myself off the field. YES! We won the toss. "Way to go Dad," I said enthusiastically as he came back to give us the lineup and positions. It was finally game time.

I walked out to home plate all clad in my armor ready to catch the first few warm up pitches from Danny, our star pitcher. The umpire looked barely older than my brother. He looked like he had never done this before, which, in the moment, felt reassuring because neither had I. He looked at me, I looked at him, and as he glanced down at the rulebook he looked at me again.

And then, he started to nervously say the words that would become a story for the ages.

"Excuse me but it says here all catchers must wear a protective cup ... so I have to ask you ... are you wearing a cup?" I looked confused, I'm sure. But he asked again, "Are you wearing a cup? It's a rule. You have to wear a cup to catch and ..."

Before he could get the rest out, I was in the dugout rummaging through the body bag to find anything that resembled what a cup may be. Afterall, I had an idea of what it was, seeing that other catchers needed to wear one. I found something I didn't recognize and knew that must be it. I shoved it in my pants and was back out there before my Dad could stop me. On my way out of the dugout I heard him say something about finding someone else to catch, that the umpire was being ridiculous with the rule. I looked at him in disbelief.

"Dad, I am the catcher … and this is my team. And I want to play, so let's play ball." I knew that if I wanted to play, I had better follow the rules. I would wear the cup just as I was told to. I didn't really care. All I knew was it was game time. It was my job to lead my team into battle.

He looked at me with big eyes and asked one more time. "Are you sure?"

I turned back to Danny and punched my hand in my glove. He threw a strike.

I think back now and wonder how long it took them to change the rulebook or to even have an awareness there was a need to consider such. But I know for sure that was one of my first defining moments. I wasn't going to let someone tell me I couldn't just because I was a girl.

In a moment that defined me, someone, somewhere needed to redefine a rule that wasn't even meant for me.

My freshman year at the University of Delaware, I took Colleen Webster's E110 class, or what most refer to as "Freshman English." I will never forget, just after chatting with my boyfriend who attended a college in New Jersey, I walked into the class that first day and saw this beautiful woman. She didn't look that much older than me, her hair long, a shade of blonde and curly. She was wearing a classic white button-down shirt. She was stunning. I was all of a sudden really interested in English. Part of what enamored me about her was the fact that she was a deep-thinker and explained things in a way that pushed me to go beyond what I was seeing and understanding of literature and writing on the surface. Yes, she was beautiful, but truthfully, she did something for me that changed my whole trajectory, and perhaps, was my defining moment number two.

I was hurrying out of class to get back to my dorm room to pack. My Dad was picking me up that evening for Thanksgiving Break, when she called to me as I had one foot out the door.

I turned abruptly and walked back in, "Yes?"

I came closer as I was wondering why she would be needing to talk to me. Then my typical fear started to bubble up: *Uh-oh, what did I do or get wrong?* My perfectionism kept that healthy or not-so-healthy fear alive for most of my life.

"Hey Jen, just wanted to wish you a great Thanksgiving Break with your family. Here's your last paper. I left you some feedback."

I watched her slide it into a manilla envelope to keep it dry from the rain that just started outside the window. I could see the pages were still a bit wrinkled from feeding it through the Brother word processor I borrowed from the red-haired girl down the hall.

"Thanks," I said, my head down looking at the way she wrote my name, her writing as free-flowing as her hair.

"What did you mention your major was?" She was staring at me while she spoke, almost perplexed.

"Uhh, psychology." I managed a slight smile, not really understanding why that mattered.

She looked at me with a serious and intense look now, and I was starting to wonder where this was going.

"You are a fantastic writer, Jen. I can't for the life of me understand why you are not doing something more with it. You have a gift, and one of the better writers I have had in my class. You should be an English major."

I think I may have stopped breathing for a moment. *What did she just say to me?* The blood rushed to my ears, causing them to flash red immediately. The introverted shyness I have carried my whole life didn't hide at all that day. I managed a "thank you" and almost stumbled out of the room.

Without a second of hesitation on my walk to my dorm, I floated instead into the Registrar's Office and changed my major. Right then and there. Five minutes from the time she recognized something in me that I doubted for so long: an ability to do something really well and, in some ways, to not be afraid to be good at something other than sports. The truth was: she saw me. Just like the high schooler, Annie, it was one of the first times in my life I had felt seen. I ended up finishing my first semester as an English major.

That paper she handed to me in the manilla envelope had these words sprawled across the top: *I was worried at first when I saw the title, and then once I read it and realized where you were going with it, I loved it. Brilliant, Jen. Keep writing. And to Jen's parents: You should be really proud. It is a pleasure to have her in my class.* Just below the handwriting was my title page: "Cleanup is a women's job …" In it, I shared "the cup story" as it has affectionately become known, and my adventures of batting in the fourth spot, or "cleanup" as the only girl on the team.

The day of the cup was definitely one of the first moments that I learned what it meant to be where my feet were. I recognized it again on my walk to the Registrar's Office to change my major, because someone I respected told me I was good enough to do so. However, it was so much more than that. It wasn't just that she told me to; what she was really saying to me that day is that she believed in me. And for a second, turning the knob of the Registrar's Office I was walking into to change my future, I believed in me too.

That belief was so much more than a superficial gain. It was a pathway to learning one of the most important things I would need for my future me: that taking action is the only way to turn a belief into knowing. As I look back, I realize it was really about taking ownership of what I wanted and stepping into the person I was to become. I just needed someone else's help to recognize her sometimes. With that, I was better able to make the best decision in each moment to move me in the direction of the person I so wanted to be.

In doing so, I have learned what it means to be fully immersed in the now. To be present. To stay in that moment and that place for whatever is needed of me. The importance of being present is not something we can really understand until we aren't present. And only then, it is so easy to see how and why we need to tune into the now. We will miss a thousand answers and a thousand moments that will change our lives if we don't learn how to be present.

Shortly after college, I worked in an office behind a desk for a large corporation. My boss's boss was a super nice guy. He just so happened to have a very quiet, monotone speaking voice. Every single morning at 8am, we had a meeting in his office to go over the day's plan. We often had meetings about having meetings. Every day, he handed out his agenda with three things on it. It always felt to me like a waste of paper. And so, every morning at 8am, with about three other people in the department, I would enter into Bob's office with one hand holding my vat of coffee, and the other, a white piece of typed up paper with usually no more than about 10 words on it.

He would begin to read it to us ... as if ... we could ... not ... read, "After taking these data points, I want you to go see Joe, and then add what he gives you and go back to Tim to get the details of what he needs for the completion of the project, and then back to me with a report from the day." His words were methodical and all of the same note and tone. I would drink my coffee as fast as possible to try to get as much caffeine as I could into my body at one time in hopes it would help my eyes stay open. What always helped however, was that on the corner of Bob's desk was a small wooden plaque that was carved. It simply said this:

## BE HERE NOW

I would read that sign every single morning as he read the agenda, almost in a desire to keep my mind in the room, each time with a different syllabic emphasis: *BE here now ... be HERE now .... be here NOW ...* "I'm sorry, what did you say?" Clearly those words were lost on me then, but they aren't lost on me now. I get the importance of being in the present moment and of truly showing up with ALL of me, ready.

One of my recent clients, a local hospital who was on the front lines during COVID-19, exhausted, frustrated, burned out and so much more, brought to life so much of what it means today to be present in the moments that truly matter. The president of the hospital at the time, Mike Duncan, wrote an email about how important it was for staff to take care of themselves and each other. He gave them support and hope in getting through that period of time to get to better days. He recognized in that moment how much we can control when we sit in the present during the hard times. His words were simple: "Be where your feet are."

In the midst of the option for digital communication through a pandemic, there were some who could NOT do their jobs through a screen. Doctors and nurses who save lives for a living, bring new lives into the world, and help ease the transition for those leaving this earth for whatever is next had no choice. While offices were empty, hospitals were overfilled. The need for understanding burnout and real empathy is just as critical as navigating around a virtual platform. Whether the digital transformation in your world has been due to a global pandemic, or one of necessity and ease of connection, this core truth remains: **Genuine connection requires more than just digital or even in-person interactions; it demands depth and intentional effort.**

And we can only get there by BEING. HERE. NOW. Aware of who and what is in front of us so we can do the next right thing that fulfills our humanness for the good of those around us.

We may have no idea what happens tomorrow, or what it will look like a year from now. That is fortune-teller business and isn't our job. We can get really good at contemplating what it looks like to have the permission to be in the now. The permission that we have been looking for our whole lives? It hasn't been from our parents, our coaches, our teachers, or our bosses … it's the permission we have been seeking from ourselves. It's the permission not to worry about what just happened or what happens next. It's the permission to be in the now.

My Dad gave me permission to find my own courage, Colleen Webster gave me the ability to take action with it, and Mike Duncan reminded me what it means to be in the moment for all of it. Courage typically doesn't show up uninvited. The only way we know how to summon it is when we are acutely aware of the need we have in the moment to do so.

Wear the cup or don't wear the cup, but whatever you do, be where your feet are. That's where the magic of true connection happens.

Trust me, you don't want to miss that.

# CHAPTER 4

# A Culture Defined by Work

According to Gallup Research, culture creates alignment. The difference lies between a team of people who are all going in different directions and a team who rallies behind a common purpose or mission. Therefore, a brand, or the way an organization wants to be known to the world, is a reflection of this alignment between the organization and its customer. Culture, like an internal brand, is then similar to how an organization wants to be known and felt by its employees.

Organizations that make promises to their customers and actually keep them are few and far between. Gallup Research states that, "only 26% of U.S. workers believe their organization always delivers on the promises it makes to customers".[1] A strong team promise and culture is very much like a strong customer promise. It must be consistent and it must build trust. When conflicting messages are being put out, it is evident that there is work to do on both sides of the equation in order to find clarity. This feeling creates misalignment not just in communication but in behaviors.[2]

Toxic work cultures will never attract the inspired, engaged, and purpose-driven employees that fuel innovation and culture. This cyclical process is one that can be mastered with the right leadership and the right people who want to help create the culture they want to live and work within. Something that is deserving of some attention and the need to be unpacked from this research is that "less than HALF of US employees (41%) strongly agree they know what their organization stands for and what makes it different from its competitors."[3] Even more so, how this will play a part in the highly competitive hiring market is key. The numbers tell us that more than 75% of the workforce will be Millenials and Gen Zers by 2025 and the desire for corporate responsibility both for diversity and social issues is an important factor for this population in choosing a job/company to work for.[4] In understanding this more deeply, let's start where we are and examine how we see these factors affecting us today.

In what is morphing into a post-pandemic world, there are so many new things to think about. Where we go from here isn't as simple as everyone jumping back into the pool after it had to be cleaned because little Johnnie had an accident. It's much deeper than that. These last four years have shown us a myriad of necessities around finding a new way of working. This can't be "back to business as usual," whatever that even means at this point. The curtain has been pulled back on exactly how people are coping right now, and how they are feeling about going back to the office after spending more than two full years at home in sweats and cozy slippers, able to sometimes better manage their family lives, in their corner of the "Brady Bunch" squares. The truth is, this has been going on for some time now, it's not a new sentiment. This version of the "American Dream" has turned into working every waking hour of the day so we can have more stuff that we don't have the time to enjoy because we are working every waking hour. The burnout is real. We are a society on the edge of collapse—a real collapse from exhaustion under the weight of the pressure to succeed.

## Meet Them Where They Are

About a year ago, my friend posted a question on Facebook about what being "out of the office" and "on vacation" really means. The question was: "When you are on vacation or have a day off from work, is it TRULY a day away from work, or does your job/boss/coworker still expect you to be accessible for work things at any time if needed?" The answers were not surprising, but were cause for awareness. When we take a "vacation" from work, whether we travel somewhere or simply stay home, do we check our email and phone messages and texts, or do we actually really step away from all of it when we take a day off. Does "off" really mean "off?" For many of the respondants on my friend's post, it does not.

Leaders who check in, stay connected, or respond to email while "on vacation" set the tone for what their work culture is. Even by sending emails at 9pm, you are showing your team that it is ok to work all hours of the day and that if you send an email then, you may also expect people to answer you then. Giving permission to yourself and your team to unplug truly may actually come back to pay dividends. If you don't, YOU may end up paying a pretty hefty price.

According to Apollo Technical, LLC, 94% of workers in the professional service industry work over 50 hours a week and 70% of all working-age people are actively looking for a job change. One of the top factors for this as of recently? Burnout.[5] According to Gallup, 77% of Americans who work full-time have experienced burnout at their jobs, with 23%, nearly a quarter, feeling it always or often.[6] Forbes published another astonishing fact: 190 billion dollars has been spent to address both the physical and psychological effects of burnout through healthcare costs, onboarding, recruitment, and turnover.[7] This isn't a problem that is going anyway anytime soon.

Asking the question, "Why is this happening?" won't solve the issue, but it certainly will give us a place to start when trying to find the solutions. Burnout isn't something that we can erase completely; there is no magic dust or secret sauce to rid the world of it like an insect that is destroying all our trees. What DOES exist is a real opportunity to do the small things that will add up to a larger positive result—the everyday, and sometimes super simple actions, we can take to get a win.

On May 26th, 2018, I boarded a flight from Newark Airport in New Jersey to Roma Fiumicino for a 10-day trip to Italy with a friend. It was one of my favorite vacations to date and one in which I learned so many important things about international culture and where we all exist within it. After landing in Rome that next afternoon, we boarded a train to *Via della Lungara* where we stayed at the Ancient Trastavere, one of the very first Airbnbs in Rome. I will never forget the huge door we entered through and once inside, leaning out the two-story open window to take in the view and breathe in the Italian air. I remember vividly what it smelled like and the oddly familiar texture of the stone wall directly across the street from our main window. The air was warm and felt like a kiss as it slowly and continuously brushed across the side of my cheek.

Everything seemed to reveal itself in slow motion around me. That forced me to work on slowing myself down and being intentional about the feeling of nothingness as I stared out the window with a glass of the most incredible Montepulciano wine in hand. I felt the sudden compulsion to NEED to breathe in every second of the beautiful history and to savor every drop of the delectable food and drink one could only fall in love with. I was immersed in incredible tastes and smells and sounds. There is no way I could have predicted how much I needed this trip.

The second day in Rome was spent sightseeing and exploring. Two of my favorite words in the world are "explore" and "adventure." This second day was surely both of them and so much more. After a short rest and a shower, we ventured back out for dinner. The streets were overflowing with people and music. It was like a movie. Everywhere

Meet Them Where They Are

I turned there was music, a young woman singing on the steps of a basilica, another playing a harp in the square, an older man playing an accordion on a folding chair next to a fountain, church bells and organs resonating through the streets. It was surreal. I realized quickly that Rome must be the place of non-stop jubilation because this was nothing more than an average Monday.

As we walked down the street, I was aware of the artistry that surrounded me, not just in paintings and murals, or statues and fountains, but in every piece of stone that was hand chiseled to become the grandiose architectural masterpieces Rome has been home to for thousands of years. As many pictures as I may have seen before of the Colosseum in Rome, I was not prepared for the way it would make me feel to stand before it as the Moon, nestled perfectly into my lens directly above the top of the building, created my own version of art history. It was a place that was, in ancient times, the host to gladiator fights and subsequent deaths of hundreds of thousands, of re-enacted ancient sea battles, and of animal hunts that brought large animals from Africa to Rome. The Colosseum was also a tie to religion, as it was often used as a Roman Catholic place of ritual, celebration and worship. It is fascinating to look back and see all of the ways it was used over time and how, even after all of these years, it is still standing and is still a cornerstone of attraction that brings people to Rome in droves.

The fascination of architecture began for me in the spring semester of 1994. I was a junior at the University of Delaware at this point and needed to take a handful of elective classes to fulfill my graduation requirements. I chose ARTH150 (Art History) Monuments and Methods as one of those classes. The professor was Dr. Wayne Craven. He happened to be a very prestigious and renowned scholar in 19th century American Art. He had published numerous books and articles and was well known as a pioneer in the world of Art History. In 1966, he started the Art History Department to stand on its own, independent from the Art Department and would go on to become a well-loved and extremely well-studied professor during my tenure on campus.

For me, professors that made the "work" feel like "play" were not as plentiful as one would desire at times. He was tough, yet his demeanor and literal romance with art was other-worldly. The way he closed his eyes when describing some of his favorite pieces and structures was not unlike the way a romance novelist would describe caressing the cheek of a beautiful woman. I was easily enamored. Not only by the beauty he taught us to see, but by my recognizing that one could love their chosen life and more so their career that deeply. In my experience it hasn't been a given to meet people like that here in the US.

According to a 2022 study by the OECD, the typical workday in Italy is 8 or 9 am until 1pm when everything closes for up to a two-hour break.[8] Work then resumes from 3pm until 6pm. The same study showed that Italy has the best work-life balance in the world, ranking 9.4 out of 10. Only 4% of full-time employees were found to have been working unhealthily long hours, whereas the average in the study was 11% across the globe. Not only is there funding for childcare for preschool children, but paid parental leave and school transport which helps to create a much healthier work-life balance for those with children. Regardless of whether or not that fits your politics, we all have to admit there is a definite appeal to having that balance.

Overall, the idea that work should be secondary to actually enjoying life to the fullest is something that is often lost in U.S. work culture. In fact, it seems to have trended toward the opposite over time. Today in America, it is a proud achievement to be the one who works the longest hours, sleeps the least and works past putting the kids to bed and even works weekends … every week.[9]

Our work structure is set up to give less vacation time, less paid time off for sickness or family needs, and to require parents to return to work faster than most European countries after giving birth. We have "perfect attendance awards" where you are actually given a plaque for NOT taking your sick time. In some situations, you can even "sell it back." What if we actually applauded the focus on self-care? Staying home when we're sick or in need of a mental health day isn't a bad thing. The American work culture is so very different from the one I saw with my own eyes at 11:17pm and 11:24pm, the time stamps on those pictures in my phone from that nighttime dinner in Roma.

I look back on the pictures of that evening often, a reminder of life from a place of joy. It was the first time I really understood why I would feel this way. It was something I that had only heard of, but could never truly picture in my own mind. *In Italy, most people work to live while in the US, most people live to work.* What a stark difference indeed. There is so much we could unpack with that one sentence and my goal is that we continue to become clearer on how we can solve this part of the problem. I think you will agree with me: we have a lot of work to do.

The way I see it is our lives are full of moments in which we are either building something or we are taking something apart. There is hardly ever a time that things just stand completely still. Every second, minute, or hour, something changes. The very cells in our bodies even change. Nothing stays the same. Time is one of the great examples of this. We will never ever get this second back, no matter how hard we want it, or how hard we try. It's gone for good. Spending time now regretting that we lost it is wasting the precious seconds in the now. It's a vicious cycle; one which we have mastered, sometimes unwillingly, but almost always unknowingly.

Those moments, those days, that week I spent immersed in a culture different from my own gave me the opportunity to see differently, to challenge my norms and typical assumptions, and asked me to show up differently. I found myself fully in tune with what I was experiencing. In fact, I don't know if I have ever felt as present as I did on that trip. I wasn't checking social media, I wasn't reading email, nor was I distracted by the TV, the news, or the like. I was completely and utterly immersed in the feeling of being in the moment and of a deeper connection to my own humanity in the midst of others. It was so different from what I had previously known. That difference would lead me into a deeper dive into examining the myth that is "work-life balance." It caused me to poke and prod around what employee engagement really is and it gave me the pause to ask a question that would be so important to my work from that moment on.

It was a February afternoon at the end of the week and I was sitting in my friend and colleague's fitness studio with a mutual friend and colleague who did similar work as me. We were discussing these issues around engagement and work-life balance and about how much employee engagement success hinges on fulfillment and how it differs in this country from others. We started to dig into what leads employees to be more engaged at their job. We had all kinds of ideas and thoughts around what that really looks like, but we came to the conclusion that as three former corporate employees (emphasis on *former*) we should probably ask people who are living it every day. My exact words were, "Well, let's meet them where they are …"

At that same moment, I logged onto Facebook and opened my personal account. I began to type; "Taking a poll: What factors lead you to be more engaged at your job?" I hit enter and pushed my laptop aside on the folding table we used as a makeshift meeting place. Bappa stood at the whiteboard as we started to jam about what we believe to be those factors. And then, the notifications began. I pulled my laptop back over in front of me and in real-time started reading them as they popped up, trying to keep up with the responses, while Bappa circled the ones we had that matched on the white board. The answers most often matched.

In just under 30 minutes, we received 74 responses to that post ... on a Friday afternoon ... at 2:30pm. Hopefully you are picking up what I am putting down. That right there would be stark realization number one. Americans are working more hours, yet are less engaged in the work—distracted by social media, life outside of the workplace, and just ... other stuff. Could there be a correlation?

Stark realization number two was that none of the responses we received had anything to do with money. Not one. They all said things like, "I want to be appreciated more, I want to feel like I belong, I am respected, and my talents are being utilized. I want to work for a company that makes a difference in the world, that has a moral compass and stands for something. I want my values and my company's values to be aligned. I want leaders who listen to me and don't talk over me, leaders who have empathy and compassion and admit when they are wrong. I want to work for a company that takes care of its people, one that I am proud to represent. I want to be a part of something bigger than me."

I can't say I was amazed at what we were seeing, and yet at the same time it felt like a certain level of validation that suddenly appeared so simply and so unapologetically. A moment I won't forget, as maybe for the first time, I really started to understand the depth of the struggle so many people are feeling in the workplace. I stared at my colleagues and then at those words that were written on that board and for a long while all three of us were silent. I sat back in my chair to take a very long, slow exhale.

"Yes," I said quietly. "This is everything."

## CHAPTER 5

# The Magic of Building Relationships

The Oxford English Dictionary defines the word "relationship" as: "the state or fact of being related" and "The way in which two things are connected."[1] Let's explore.

At the end of it all, we won't wish we had more things, or worry about how many boats or cars or bank accounts we collected in our lifetimes. We will look back on the ways in which we were connected and spent our time in community with others. It is most assuredly the people, the time we spent with them, and the relationships we built that will consume our last thoughts. It is all about the state of being connected. Really, truly connected.

Really great leaders get this to varying degrees, but not always completely. They know they may need to do more of it in order to be successful and they know it's important. The *best* leaders build relationships, not out of necessity, but desire. The truth is clear: the outcome is that inspired, engaged, and purpose-driven leaders are more likely to have employees that move the needle on creativity and innovation. Those people who feel connected and who are living their lives on purpose see the magic in building strong and healthy relationships. Everything is interconnected and each piece can't thrive without the others.

I have heard from so many how hard it is to be creative at work. Diversity of thought helps to fuel creativity which helps to fuel innovation. In an article about this very idea, Gallup states that 35% of employees are only given the time to be creative or to discuss new ideas once or twice a year, if that.[2] Even more telling is that only 18% say they feel safe taking risks with this power at all.[3] I wonder how often leaders actually remind their employees of the importance of thinking, of exploring new ideas and new ways of doing things, or of the power of connection and community. We can't grow unless we find value in the growing, and we can't build relationships unless we build the trust and the safety to do so.

I saw this first hand when I was a little girl. My Mom loved to explore, looking for hidden treasures. However, instead of the sunken pirate ship looking for a chest of gold, she would explore antique stores for older china or furniture that someone else moved on from. As a young girl, I often was roped into going along. Really, what choice did I have? Every time, regardless of where we were or how long we planned to stay, Mom would start up a conversation with the owner, the shopkeeper, or just the random worker behind the counter. By the time I was tugging on her sleeve to finally get out of there, she knew where they were from, what their family and friend tree looked like, what they liked to do on Sundays, and what their favorite soup recipe was. She also would share her story, about her husband and her kids, and the interesting facts about the small town she grew up in. And I do mean every time. She didn't leave until she honestly made a new friend.

We used to tease her because she would talk to a wall, if she thought it would hold a conversation with her. She had the gift of gab, we called it. What I realize now is that wasn't the *real* gift she possessed. Yes, she could talk for a long time, but that isn't what was remarkable about her in this way. Her *real* gift is that she knew how to listen and be present, and in that same vein, she in turn, knew how to connect and build relationships. In doing so, she built a community around her that was strong, and it seemed effortless.

When I was given the 2009 Female Business Leader of the Year Award, I used this idea as the focal point of my acceptance speech. I was asked to say a few words about my success and how I got to where I was at the time. I made it clear that one of the things I knew, beyond a shadow of a doubt, was that building relationships is the ONLY way to build a business. In fact, I think this is where my very tagline came from:

*"Because we aren't meant to do this alone."*

The moment a client walked through our door to the moment they walked out, our first and most important goal was to make sure they felt like they belonged there, and that they were the most important person in the entire universe at that moment. We made it a point to put everything down when someone would walk in. We wanted them to know that they were the only thing that mattered. I make it very clear everywhere I go that I am invested in the work I do and with whom I do it. Building relationships with my clients therefore is an essential piece to walking the talk. So why is it important for businesses to build relationships? Because a company's greatest asset will always be its people and the best way we function is in the community of others.

I gave a talk at my local library back in 2014 after my first book was published. It was there that I met Julie. She was 93 years old and happened to be working that evening as the greeter at the front desk.

We struck up a conversation and I found out quickly that she lived in the same complex as me. We talked and talked and talked. I left that night with her phone number and address. She had invited me over to her place for a glass of wine.

Julie and I shared red wine and Fritos often and I got to learn all about her past as one of the first women to hold the position she did in the US Marine Corp. I also found out she wrote poems, but not just any poems. She mastered the art of the limerick. One of her prized possessions was a letter from Michelle Obama thanking her for the limerick she sent for the First Lady's birthday. It was proudly framed on the wall by the front door next to a picture of Julie in her uniform. One of the last times I got to see Julie before I moved, she wrote me my very own limerick and gave it to me to keep. It started with the words:

> **"There once was a gal named Jen**
> **Who wrote of her life with a pen …"**

I have never forgotten Julie or the memories of our hours and hours of laughter and conversation. We created a lasting connection from one simple moment. My life is forever richer for that one pivotal decision where we chose to engage in a hello in the lobby of the Chester County library.

As we talk about building relationships, it is critical to mention the different leadership styles that have been studied over the past 100 years. The first three styles were defined by Social Psychologist, Kurt Lewin, in 1939: Autocratic, Democratic, and Laissez-Faire.[4] In 1947, Sociologist Max Weber coined the term "Transactional Leader," while exploring three different categories leaders can fall into: Legal, Rational, and Authority. Nearly three decades later in 1973, James V. Downton studied the concept of "Transformational Leadership" and in 1985, Bernard M. Bass brought this idea to life by finding ways in which it showed up and expanding the success of it.[6] Transformational Leadership is the cornerstone of how my team and I built out our B.R.A.V.E. Human Leadership framework. Transformational leaders lead with compassion, innovation, and inspiration at the forefront and are fantastic change agents through a strong culture of authenticity and empathy.

How we view the importance of relationships plays an important role in how we lead. It matters when focusing on a people-centric mission and vision. The best way to do that is to take a deeper look into how we build relationships that fulfill us. What are we doing to make sure we are connecting in ways that will bring a real sense of belonging to the people in our circle? In turn, that sense of belonging in a relationship in order to build a community that is strong and difficult to be broken. In theory, this sounds like an everyday, simple enough question. Sometimes those are the ones that are, in fact, the hardest to answer.

---

**CASE STUDY**

Brian Wanner, Former Vice President, Human Resources—Giant Food

---

*Jen*: Brian, thanks for spending time answering these questions for me. I know your background lends itself to helping us understand the power of relationships and how trust plays a role here. What can you tell us about your experience with these factors?

*Brian*: I have been in the retail food industry for over 25 years and have been in my current role for over two years. Overall, my time in the industry has been split equally between HR and several other functions including Operations, Operations Support, Supply Chain, Innovation/Optimization, and a small stint in Merchandising.

I feel my cross-functional experience is critical to helping me understand the business, and how it operates while being able to better understand my peer's responsibilities and challenges. That is even more critical in my current role leading the HR function for the Giant Food brand.

Trust is the most important aspect of building a relationship. I want someone to be able to trust me, my team, and the entire HR function. I don't believe there is much that can be accomplished without having the trust in any type of relationship.

First, I understand that trust takes time, and everyone's approach to trust is different. Some people will provide trust upfront while others need to see if your actions match your words before they give you trust. Ultimately, I need to understand that it is my responsibility to earn the trust of others.

For me, there are four key elements that I strive to demonstrate in building trust. First is to always be truthful and provide transparency which includes taking time to explain the why or my intentions. The second is to ensure that I do what I say we will do and if something happens that it can't be done, I need to proactively communicate and provide an update. The third is to listen and absorb what is being said, do I understand what someone is telling me and can I put myself in their shoes to understand why it is important to them? Finally, to be aligned. We may not completely agree with each other, but we understand and hear each other including the why/intent of each other.

Leading the HR function is critical to have trust and alignment. My goal as an HR team with my peers and the organization is to "Deliver solutions that enable the organization's talent to grow while actively contributing to the overall business results and support a culture of care."

───※───

While leaders like Brian don't exist in every single organization, it would be so much more beneficial if they did. These are the **Relational Leaders** that understand the value of culture, leading with empathy, and building a community of practitioners to help in this work. They will always be more effective leaders than those who don't make these behaviors a priority. You will read more about Relational Leaders later in the proprietary research we conducted on this topic.

Building relationships is an art. It can be learned. Much like throwing a ball, adding nine plus four, and spelling the word *antidisestablishmentarianism*. And it takes work. Typically, it doesn't happen in your car alone or during moments you are not in tune with those around you. It takes the work of actually going out and building strong bridges that can span the gaps that exist between us, building structures that will last. Structures that will often lead to deeper connections and stronger communities.

# CHAPTER 6

# The Compelling Case for Compassion

Here is how 2023 began for my family:

- February 23rd: my Dad died.
- February 25th: I officiated at my brother's wedding in NYC.
- March 18th: I delivered the eulogy at my Dad's memorial service.
- May 19th: I said MY OWN vows as I married my best friend in front of 140 of our closest friends and family members.

In less than three short months, I had known and seen and felt the highest of highs and the lowest of lows. To say the roller coaster ride was extreme would be an understatement. And yet, looking back now I recognize these moments as just facets of my human experience and I know so many of you can relate.

It is hard sometimes to really see the whole picture when you are truly just focused on getting through each second as it happens. Each moment swirls us around like the universe just gave our huge glass a very vigorous stir. David C. Baker once said "You can't read the label from inside the jar."[1] It often takes others to remind us the jar even has a label or to read the fine print when you forgot your glasses. This all takes a whole lot of grace and compassion, not just for ourselves, but for each other. That connection is the thread that will always weave us all together. It's something that we need to survive. It's the power of building relationships and true connections.

We, as a society, are CRAVING connection. Loneliness is no longer being laughed at as a research topic: it is now considered an epidemic by psychologists around the globe.[1] The only way to begin to uncover the true solutions to this problem is to foster more conversations around compassion and belonging. The key here, however, is to make sure we recognize those around us in this work: Who is taking over the conversation and who is being left out? Where can we invite others in? Where can we leave gaps and openings to do so?

Why do I believe people are generally NOT okay during the recent past? Because they've told me, and even more so, because I have felt it myself. It's been a long, hard road these past few years and yet understanding how we connect with others and that our need to do so is embedded in our very DNA, may be a way to remind ourselves of what's important NOW. In the end, perhaps a collective deep breath is our next best and next right thing to do. We don't have to take a whole FULL step forward, all we need is to LEAN forward and we can be sure of one truth: we are not moving backward. In fact, we can NEVER go back in time. It's just not possible. We have not really managed to figure that out yet. All we can do is stay still or move forward knowing that if we stand still, time still goes on without us. This is the hardest part of forward movement: the understanding that in order to do so, the only thing we can ever be is present. Being able

## Meet Them Where They Are

to move forward, or move on is about being present in every moment. Navigating that can be one of the hardest things we ever do.

We NEED each other now for connection, grace, hope, compassion, empathy, and love. That is our human need for control. In order to obtain that, we need to give all of that to ourselves first. We need to put ourselves at the top of the list and in no uncertain terms, understand WHY.

NO, this isn't another conversation about loving yourself before anyone else can, or you get what you give, putting oxygen masks on, etc. What I mean is this: we NEED each other to survive. And the only way to make sure we stay connected is to give that same grace and compassion and love and empathy to ourselves.

The truth is, no matter how much you may hope, no one is coming to save you. YOU are the one you've been waiting for. Ironic, isn't it? I wrote this book to center around the need for each other and to discuss the importance of community and connection. While that is at the core of what will move us forward, it has to start somewhere. And truthfully? I think we all could use a brush-up on the self-love and respect goal. The problem starts when we wait for someone else to do it for us so we don't have to get that uncomfortable and look too closely at all the stuff we don't like about ourselves. No one is coming to do it for us. If we had known that all along, would we have always still waited for someone to come along? Like sitting at the bus stop when you KNOW the last bus already came and left an hour before ... and still you sit and you wait anyway, thinking *NO ... there HAS to be another one. I don't believe that was the last bus.* Even when I KNOW it was the last? Have I been sitting here waiting for a bus that was never coming?

In some ways, I think we have become too afraid to rely on our own intuition or feelings, and look to others to change us or to make it better. We rely on technology, parents, and bosses to tell us what to do next or what directions to take. What happens when we lose that very thing we have been relying on? Let me tell you exactly what happens then: you panic and wonder what you did before you had it.

It was a Tuesday morning in August, and I was rolling my carry-on suitcase with my backpack attached to it out to my driveway where my driver, John, stood waiting. We exchanged our pleasant greetings, as always, as he grabbed my luggage and put it in the back of the black Chevy Suburban. I grabbed the "oh shit" handle as I climbed up into the SUV. I always feel like I am part of the Secret Service or something like it when I am riding in the back of these vehicles. I laugh, adjusting my shades on the bridge of my nose.

"Where are you headed this time, Jen?" he asked. John always likes to hear about my business travel, and the companies and work I am doing while hurrying to different parts of the country. We usually talk the whole 40-minute ride to the airport and talk about work, family, hobbies, and the deeper things that life gives us to share with each other. I have grown to consider him a friend.

As usual, the time flew by and just before we pulled up in front of Terminal B for American Airlines. I started to get that panicked feeling grow from my feet all the way up to the top of my head. "Oh no!" I said loudly and without letting John say a thing. I said quickly, "I think I left my cell phone at home." His immediate response was to look at the clock and ask if we had enough time to turn back to get it. We both realized we would never make it back in time to board the flight, so I would need to go without it. He pulled over and had me type a text to anyone I could to have them ship my phone priority overnight to my hotel room in Erie, PA that I would be arriving at in the next two hours. We figured the best thing was to have it shipped so I could get it there the next morning. We said goodbye and he was on the text thread with my family and friends to coordinate "Operation

Find-and-Ship-Jen's-Phone" before I was even in the air. I adore that man. He is exactly the kind of person I would want in customer-facing relationships for my company. John has been a treasure I have found just because I was in need of car service to the airport for business trips.

I walked into the airport doors and the whole list of things that was about to be difficult without my phone started to trickle through my brain like a CVS receipt. It was long. SO, first thing's first. I began to think as if it was 1995 and I had just graduated college. First thing ... go to the ticket counter and print a boarding pass. A WHAT?? Yes! They still print cardstock tickets. I walked up and the woman greeted me right away.

"Do you have your boarding pass?"

I looked at her and slowly smiled. "No. That is why I am here."

She next asked for my ticket locator number, "You can scan your phone here and I can look it up."

"Uhhh I don't have my phone, that's the issue. I need my paper ticket printed please."

Not surprisingly, she looked at me funny. "OHHH," she said. "That's hard."

I laughed and said, "I know," as if I had ANY idea how hard it would actually be.

The actual flight to Buffalo went off without a hitch: 43 minutes from takeoff to touchdown. All good there. When I landed and started to walk toward the AVIS counter, I cringed again. All of my information was on my phone. I assumed however that they could just look me up when I showed them my ID.

As I approached the counter a woman with a smile and kind eyes asked if she could help me. I gave her my name and she said, "Ok, great, you're Avis Preferred. You are all set, here is the key."

And then I interrupted her. It hit me that I had no idea where I was and where I was going. "DO you have a GPS unit?" I cringed thinking I knew the answer and while she looked under the counter a few times and then said they don't have them anymore. I started to feel that rush again over my body. "HMMM … OK … that's going to be an issue," I said out loud. She looked back at me puzzled.

"I usually just use the Apple CarPlay on my phone," she explained to me slowly, almost in awe that I may have never heard of it.

I laughed, "Well … yes, me too. Except I left the APPLE part of that at home."

It took her a minute to register what I just said, and she smiled with a quiet "duh" chuckle as soon as she did. I knew that my hotel wasn't close to the airport so I couldn't even really guess.

She was deep in thought and then stopped and said, "Wait … let me see something." She hurried over to the white SUV that was parked out front and started to take things out. She looked back at me and said I could take the car she had been driving because it had GPS built in. "It will just be a few minutes if you are ok with that. I just need to get my stuff out and transfer it to a different car and then get it cleaned."

I thanked her as she was taking out a car seat and coloring books and moving them from one vehicle to the other as quickly as she could. It was at that moment that I realized that maybe not having my phone wasn't really a bad thing. It was a challenge, sure, but it also forced me to take a closer look at how I navigate the world and how I have spent so much time needlessly scrolling and, therefore, awfully disconnected from the world at arm's length. What might come from a self-imposed phone break once a month. A full day without it ... turned off and put away. Those 24 hours without my phone brought a new appreciation for people and for connection.

See, we NEED each other. We are made for connection with others, just like our lives have grown easier with technology ... AND ... we can't rely on others to do the hard stuff or to tell us how to heal our heavy hearts right now. Both things can be true and I think in the midst of this balance is where we find ourselves. Where we realize that everything is really going to be ok.

Except for the times we struggle to believe our own happy story we sell. And that, that is what will make or break us. You, me, them ... we all have a story.

Put a fire in, pour a cup, and grab a blanket.

It's about to get real ...

## CHAPTER 7

# Through Broken Pieces We Mend

I have written about a lot of topics over my almost 51 years on this planet. From what I was going to have for lunch in first grade, to boy and girl crushes in a journal in eighth grade, to love, to heartbreak, to sports, to business, to 45-page capstone thesis papers, to erotic poetry, to articles for the newspaper, to mental toughness workbooks, to blogs that became a book, to commencement speeches, to both my parents' eulogies, and to a suicide note I never delivered. To this ... Book Two. I have written all of it. This truth may be the one that has saved my life.

For so long, I have listened and watched as the world would get dark and then lighten. I was pretty sure it looked like the natural progression of a 24-hour, like what everyone else imagined was happening while they were asleep. But mine was often really long and really drawn out. Sometimes it would last for days. Some days felt and looked like nights ... some nights like days. Most times the dark was like an underwater cave and I was drowning in it because I couldn't breathe and couldn't find the opening to get out.

When I was in high school, I had a breakdown. I ran away from home. My parents worried. I am not exactly sure why I did it, but when I walked through the door after two days of not being able to find me, they accepted me with open arms, held me, and we all cried. They cried because I scared them. They didn't know what was going on and didn't understand why I would do that. I cried and didn't even know why. That was the night they decided I would make my first trip to see a psychologist. They wanted to help me. They didn't know. I didn't know. We were hoping someone would know something.

I remember the feeling like it was yesterday, my knees hitting the floor while I wailed. I felt tormented and couldn't understand what could possibly be so bad at the age of 16. Several years later I chalked up my angst and my impossible happiness as teenage hormones and my confusion over my sexual identity. Over the years I came out as gay, lesbian, and finally settling into what feels more authentically me … bisexual. I don't hide my identity yet it's not *the* definition of me. It's just a part of me. It's in a long list of words that would describe who I am. It's just a small piece of my story.

I have experienced deep love and profound loss, holding them both in the same hands at a young age. My first love when I was 13, my first loss long before. They continued to weave in and out of my existence. Like most people, I have had pierced both my heart and my breath deeply. Like Velcro that is mixed with super glue, they are strong and unforgiving. They bind my claustrophobic self in that cave, underwater, not able to find my way out. And so it continued …

I chalked everything up to grief, or sadness, or "I just feel deeply," and I moved on. I wrote about it, in not so many words. I often wondered why the pain sometimes was so sharp and other times so dull I didn't feel a thing. I shrugged it off as just being human, well … because I am.

In my late 20s, an almost 10-year relationship ended. I felt like a failure. I wasn't worthy of happiness or love. That must be it. I caused infidelity in our relationship. I caused her pain. I ruined everything. And just like that I was back on my knees. Helpless. In tears. Yet it felt normal. It felt like what "should" happen when love ends. However, the thoughts that came next were much like the ones that I wrote about in my journal when my tormented self ran away from home. I was now exposed. I wanted to run away from everything, except this time never come back. For the second time, this time more sincerely, I contemplated ending my life. I remember the trip to the local CVS to buy a notebook to write in my car. It was then that I penned what would be a suicide note. I just couldn't handle the pain. It was so deep. I hurt so much it felt like it would never stop. It was then also that my Mom was diagnosed with the disease that would take her away from us 13 years later. It was then, just after my breakup and Mom's diagnosis, that I had to put my dog Zoe down. The one living being that kept me from ever really being alone. It was just too much. I wasn't capable of handling it all at once.

I sought out counseling for the second time in my life. This time they gave me meds that I took for one day and had me see a Cognitive Behavior Therapist. I would do that for a few months until I felt like I was good enough and I had spent enough money that I didn't have at the time. I walked away feeling ok. Alone and more hollow than before, but ok.

That thread would be constant. In a world where I was surrounded by lots of people, those that surround me daily, and those that have become family, to my DNA family and the people I know casually, there are times I felt intense loneliness. Even the 20+ years of my life I have spent in serious committed relationships. It wasn't always them. It isn't always the friends and family that surround me. I have come to recognize it's a part of what this is all about. It's part of my story.

I have been in moments where I was surrounded by a whole slew of people and have felt the most alone, I have ever felt. I have laid in bed next to someone and felt like I was a mile away. I have felt deeply and at the same time was completely numb.

In my 30s, I would contemplate suicide again. I once again got in my car and left. This time for a few days, I disappeared from the world and all who loved me. I was ashamed and sad. I had failed again and felt like I wasn't good enough to deserve happiness. I now believed deep down I never would be. I wasn't coming back. I didn't care anymore. Finally, my brother got through to me. All of a sudden, I realized I was hurting everyone around me. I honestly didn't want that. Of course, I knew that, but when you are in the middle of such pain, you don't see anything clearly. You just want the pain to end, the cave closes in once more, and that's it. That's why people do it. For all those who wonder how people can die by suicide, it's certainly not clear cut and simple. It's not easily understood unless you are standing in the midst of this underwater cave that has no opening. You can't breathe. You can't explain it to those who are carrying oxygen tanks around wondering why you don't just borrow theirs. In the minds of those who are suffering, it's not actually a selfish thing … it feels selfless in the moment. If I take away my suffering, it will be easier for those around me to not have to deal with me or feel pain because of me.

When you stand on the outside and look in, it's so much easier to see the obvious flaws with that idea. As I have written of my turmoil above, from the logical brain, it feels "dramatic and somewhat ridiculous." I have heard those words from loved ones and those with whom I have shared my bed. I know they meant well. They just didn't know. How could they? Neither did I.

And so, I finally found my calling. I found what I was meant to do with my life. They say those who struggle with something often make that their life's mission. So it was with me. I think I became good at giving others inspiration and hope because I needed to find it for myself. If my life had a purpose that was bigger than me, I think, in some ways, it gave me a reason. It has caused me to embrace my struggles more authentically and come to terms with the fact that my story is just like so many others' stories and that's not a bad thing. I think it is what has made me relatable.

I was devastated and hurt and felt deep pain and struggle when my Mom died the day after Christmas in 2013 and shortly after when another relationship ended very painfully. I once again was in that underwater cave. And yes, my mind would wonder about what I could do to just stop the pain. I fought it this time with everything I had. I went to counseling for the third time and finally started to actually take the meds I was once again prescribed. This time I let go of the "strong" routine. I stopped worrying about what people would think. I started to embrace the fact that this is real life for me; that I needed to learn to handle loss and grief and not spiral out of control each time I started to feel it; that if I continued to find my way into the underwater cave over and over again, at some point, I may not make it out. In fact, I knew I wouldn't.

I have listened to stories of some of my heroes in my field. They have bared their souls, shown cuts and scrapes and bruises, and oftentimes allowed us to see them bleed, cry, and be human. That is what makes them so good. There have been many people who said creatives usually have a dark and tormented side. Who knows if that's true but if it is I understand it. As authentic as I have always tried to be, I realized that this is a part of my story that has remained silent. Not necessarily on purpose but just because I haven't actually sat and put words around it. Today, for some reason, it felt right. Probably because once again, we have watched icons and stars and brilliant people who felt a whole lot of pain and could never escape that underwater cave leave this Earth because it was just too hard to find their way out time and time again. I have listened to people mourn them. I have watched as people wondered why. "How could they?" they ask, "They seemed so happy and alive. I don't understand …" I have quietly understood the pain and the desire and the angst. I have lived through that torment. The only difference is I was lucky enough to find my way out somehow each time.

Depression is unyielding. It is silent. It sneaks up sometimes when you least expect it. It is unforgiving. It doesn't care who you are or what you do for a living. It doesn't care about your social status, age, religion, sexuality or what you have in your bank account. The list is long of those who had a long-standing debt to its long thread from which none of us can escape: Ernest Hemingway, Kurt Cobain, Robin Williams, Chris Cornell, Chester Bennington, Naomi Judd, Anthony Bourdain, Kate Spade, Avicii, and Stephen Boss. And that only scratches the surface of some names we know.

There may never be a satisfactory answer to the dominant question of "why?" There is nothing anyone could want to hear that could possibly soothe their heart after learning of such a tragic ending. Nothing will bring them back or make it better. Nothing. The only real answer we have is that depression is a tricky disease. One I know all too well. So, this is my authentic life. I have struggled with anxiety and depression since I was young. I haven't put words to it and I haven't spoken about it because it was just a part of my story, but it IS part of my story and one that I need to tell.

Maybe I am writing this chapter for the same reason I wrote my first book, because I just needed to put words to it for me. It's how I have learned to handle the hard things: put words to it, understand it, embrace it, and if someone else is better for it, then that is a good secondary result.

I know the pressure I feel is from no one but myself. I never wanted anyone to doubt my ability to do my job. To deliver something important and powerful and intelligent. To be a good and whole partner. To be a stable and fun friend. There is such a stigma around depression. I never wanted to appear weak. While feeling that, I realized that I am part of that exact problem. My silence does NO ONE any good. The stigma exists because we don't talk about it and we certainly haven't done a good job putting a face to it. Mental health is not always scary or ugly. It doesn't always look like the disheveled mess on the street corner or the quiet neighbor that kept to themselves and never left the house. It's not always wrapped up in tears or sadness or silence. It looks like your dad, your sister, your boss, your doctor, your best friend, your partner. It looks like me.

Included with my master's degree, my love of life, my sense of humor, my ability to love deeply, my friendships, my passion, my creativity, my sexuality, my drive to inspire, my fun, my crazy wild side are all parts of me … so is depression and anxiety. This is just a part of my story.

Whether or not it's part of yours too, I know for sure you know someone who can relate to this.

The true power is in being able to talk about it.

It is time to put words to it. For me and maybe for you.

This is my realization that even through the hard times, I am ok.

I am ok.

Actually, I am better than ok.

And, in fact, recognizing that doesn't make me weak in the least.

I used to think that I was broken, that being whole and finding true happiness was a fairytale. But the truth is, we find in vulnerability real strength. I am, in fact, not broken. Having depression isn't about being less than whole any more than having blue eyes or being right-handed or being five foot eleven is. It isn't *the* definition of who I am. This is a part of my story and perhaps within that story, I recognize that I am not what's broken. Maybe it's the perception that we have to be perfect to be successful, or we have to have certain things, or be certain kinds of people to be loved.

Life has felt authentically shattered at times: sparkling and dancing under the streetlamps at times, laughing uncontrollably at midnight, quietly sitting in the silence of grief at daybreak, with the realization that through broken pieces, we mend. Even in those moments when the nights seem to never end and the days drag on, the beat in your chest races then fades away. Little by little there is a faint, dim light that keeps fading too and your only hope now is that it doesn't go all the way out. You pull, it tugs. You let go at the wrong time. Timing is everything. No matter what you do, you just can't pull it all back together. Being human includes broken pieces. The ones that shatter or break into a million smaller ones. The pieces you don't even know if you can find to put all back together again. It includes the pieces that break in half or thirds, and sometimes, the ones that crack, that you can just start to see the separation but don't come all the way apart.

There are a thousand ways to break something. Big or small, it feels broken. Scratched. Damaged. And through those broken pieces we mend. We find out how strong we are when we figure out how to keep it together ... when we don't want anyone to see, when we are vulnerable and real and authentic. Like the Velveteen Rabbit, being real doesn't mean you are perfect ... quite the contrary.[1] Being real means that you are loved, and your parts are worn and oftentimes tattered.[2] Being real means you break, maybe not in a million pieces, but perhaps in thirds. As you break, so can you mend.

There is a tradition in Japan called Kintsugi or Kintsugari. This is when a piece of ceramic breaks or cracks, and the repair technique is to cover those cracks and breaks by repairing them with gold or silver or platinum to highlight the cracks. There is a beauty in the broken, and the Japanese see the joining of the pieces back together as part of the ceramic's history ... part of its journey, not something to cover up, hide, and be embarrassed about. In a society that throws broken things away, what a beautiful idea to see something for what it is and find the beauty in all of it. To mend the broken pieces with something even more aesthetically pleasing and valuable than the ceramic piece was in its original form.[3]

Just like the moments that create our path, the stories we tell ourselves, the broken parts we feel we are made of ... to embrace those parts for the beauty they hold, to make them more beautiful for the fact that they are broken, and to mend them by "joining" the pieces, not in trying to "fix" them. This is the beauty in the imperfection of our own humanity. It's the recognition of the value we hold. This compassion and awareness to the things we don't control, to that which is outside ourselves, and to those pieces we hold onto and can't seem to let go of, is the gold that holds us together. It's the love that joins us and does not throw us away for being broken. Perhaps the truth is we aren't broken at all, and therefore need no fixing. We are all just pieces of ourselves, that when highlighted in gold are so much more beautiful for being real and authentic.

We know we are worthy of so much more when we are real. When we break and join back together. When we see ourselves for what we are in all of our vulnerability, even when we feel broken.

It is through those broken pieces that we mend. We become more and more beautiful each time.

Each one of us. Together. This is my story, and maybe even yours too. I want to get really good at telling it. It's what will keep me connected to a community of human beings all just trying to do our best. I see you. I am you. And I will sit in the fire with you for as long as it takes to heal …

**… *because we aren't meant to do this alone.***

# PART II

## CHAPTER 8

# B.R.A.V.E. and the Five Words

Let's start at the beginning. I spent much of my early career in sports. Softball was my first love. I played the game for 42 years of my 51+ year life thus far. As I write this book, it is only the second year that I willingly didn't pick up my glove and dust off my cleats. Who is to say when it's enough, but I decided I had other priorities I was excited about like my beautiful home and my gardens. I sit outside and admire them often while spending time with my wife and pups.

During those 42 years, I also spent about 12 of them coaching the sport in some way. Four at the high school level, three at the college level, and one year at the pro level while running camps and clinics throughout all 12 years. During that time, I earned a certification in Mental Game Coaching and attended workshops with a well-known sports psychologist in Florida, Dr. Patrick Cohn. I felt like I had tapped into a whole new way to coach and a whole new way to understand performance that involved not only improving skills and technique, but to really focus on the mental side of the game. When asked, most athletes will tell you the mental aspect of sports is more important than all of the physical skills combined. When harnessed properly, the correct mentality can catapult a middle of the road athlete into a champion.

When I came onto the scene as a motivational speaker, I built the first part of my speaking career on what I called the "Five C's." I still stand by the fact that they are the foundation for overall belief in your performance, and the success gained in showing up as your best self. Those five C words are: Character, Communication, Choice, Courage and Confidence. Throughout that work and research, this is what I found: The brain creates pathways of repetition in sports we call routines and when followed, will always bring an athlete back to center, or to being grounded quickly. After a mistake, a doubt ,or a negative thought, we can actually train the mind to focus on the right things for success.

Through that notion, *there was something that just worked about creating a five-word mantra.*

It was just long enough without taking too much time to repeat in the middle of competition. It would become the catalyst to everything else I have done since then. If you notice here, just like in my first book, every chapter title is five words and every acronym I use is five letters, which in turn is composed of five different words. It was during a moment of this conversation that follows when and how "The Five Words" were born.

In 2013, during Spring Training Baseball in Florida, my client Matt had reached out to me before a game to get a confidence boost as a way to help him focus and stay positive as he was called up to the Big League stage that year. He had asked me to give him "something" to go into that day with—some kind of reassurance. Without hesitation, I asked him why he played baseball. As soon as the words left my mouth, I was worried he would think it was a dumb question, but he responded right away.

"I play because I love it."

And right then, I realized there was something to that. I replied, "for love of the game."

"Yes, that's it!" Matt said smiling. I could hear it in his voice.

That was the day my five-word mantras started, and they continue today, from my own daily mantras, to the titles of these book chapters, to the title of the book itself. I have seen others use the five words to find their mantra too. It. Just. Works.

Let's fast forward to B.R.A.V.E. and how we got here. When I transitioned a lot of my work to the corporate world, it took off and as it did, I decided that the concept of the Five C's needed a deeper dive. I was starting to spend a lot of time studying how leadership and culture feed off of each other. I began to wonder if there was a way to really make a difference with words. I read a lot about inclusive leaders and how cultures of belonging were really the most important part of this work. In fact, the story was quite grim. As I mentioned, loneliness was a huge topic, and the words "diversity, equity and inclusion" (DEI) became whole departments. After the deaths of George Floyd, Breonna Taylor, and Tamir Rice, most companies who didn't have DEI teams before, were frantically creating them.

The hard part, however, was that most of these companies wanted to make sure they were on the right side of the ledger when consumers started to scrutinize who was taking this issue seriously and who was not. Those who were paying attention worked hard to make sure the words were not just lip service. There had to be action that followed closely behind. Just like anything else we have seen in the beginning phases when something is new, so many had no clue what they were doing. I think most I have spoken to about this have said that in the beginning, doing something felt better than doing nothing, however as time went on, it was quite clear that opening the scabs of what is often a really difficult topic for many was sometimes doing more harm than good. It was imperative to get this right. Listening, seeking to understand, wanting to make sure we did things that helped and not hurt the very people we wanted to lift up was what made B.R.A.V.E. Human Leadership even an idea. When we got down to it, there was a problem that needed to be solved and it went deeper than we understood. We know that we all have different life experiences. I will NEVER know what it is like to be a black woman, or a trans man, or anyone other than who I am. Through our work in this space, we have had the opportunity to listen to the stories and lived experiences of so many who have felt "othered" in their workplace. What we heard over and over was that real cultural change doesn't come from one speaker during Black History Month or a rainbow sticker during Pride Month. So, where DOES real change come from? This is what brings us to what we call the Five C's 2.0:

1. **Curiosity.** To ask the difficult questions about biases, discrimination, gaps, etc. Even just to understand how the day-to-day impacts those who don't feel like they belong. How does this impact their engagement or their ability to show up as the only (insert race, sex, color, national origin, gender identification, religion, age, different abilities, sexual orientation, or veterans status, etc. here).

2. **Clarity.** By asking the questions and listening to the answers, blind spots will inevitably be revealed.

3. **Commitment**. This is where we have seen organizations get stuck in the "Let's skip to the good part" scenario. There is no shortcut to cultural change and it must be embraced and demonstrated from the top down.

4. **Consistency.** You can't go to the gym once and expect to walk out a bodybuilder.
5. **Culture.** In order to get here, you have to do 1 through 4.

Of all the intersections that make up who we are, our most important thread is that we are woven together as people and it is to celebrate, not fear our differences. B.R.A.V.E. Human Leadership was never intended to be a DEI model. What it did aim to do however, was to try to help bridge a gap we saw when organizations jumped haphazardly toward action without trying to critically examine their culture and the leadership behaviors that would be necessary to sustain or change it. To that end, my team and I recognized that by building B.R.A.V.E. cultures we can help DEI initiatives work WITH an organization, not AGAINST it.

A growth mindset begs us to stay open to all of it and is, in and of itself, critical to us moving forward. As we emerge from the rubble of where we have been these past few years, we have the chance to do it better. I often recognize that within the most heightened chaos comes some of the most change-making opportunities. The opportunities to grow and evolve into our best selves are ours to embrace. This hasn't been a typical, normal stretch of time. We have faced many challenges as human beings that we have been asked to rise above time and time again. We have also realized more today than ever before, is that best practices in leadership must be people-centric. The tide that will take us forward must focus on lifting ALL people.

In early 2024, JLynne Consulting Group and the Human Leadership Institute partnered with independent research firm Audience Audit to formally study how leaders think and feel about their role, purpose, and approach to leading others. This research has allowed us to dive into the exact questions we wanted answered using attitudinal or psychographic segmentation, which is based on the belief that leaders with shared beliefs or attitudes tend to have the same behaviors. With this method, the research would give us never-before-seen insights into these bold humans doing vital work in our society.[1]

There were no demographic or organizational factors that determined the mindsets, it was really all about attitudes of the leader. From February to April 2024, 214 full-time employees with managerial, leadership, or administrative responsibilities and who manage others, participated in our survey, providing us with timely and relevant data. The figure below depicts the four types of leaders that emerged from the survey. The leader type we recognize to be the strongest amongst both the performance axis as well as the people axis, is what we've called the "Relational Leader." This segment was only 19% of our respondents overall. The other three segments were "Constrained Leaders," our highest respondent category at 32%, "Outcome-Oriented Leaders," 26%, and "Emotionally-Oriented Leaders," 23%.[2]

Figure 8.1: Types of Leaders

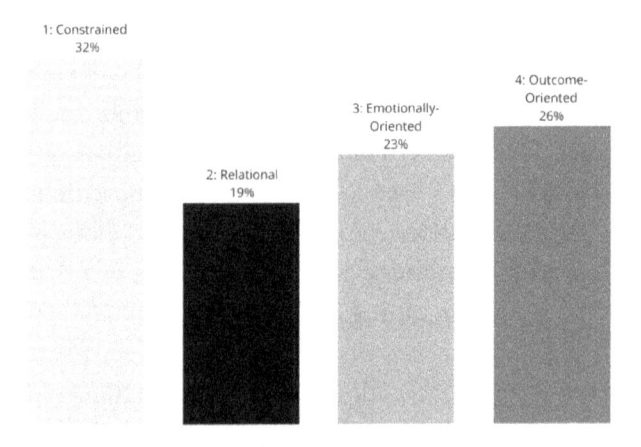

Note: Audience Audit, & Human Leadership Institute. (2024, September). How B.R.A.V.E. Human Leadership Behaviors Define Relational Leaders: Leading With Mind and Heart. https://www.thehli.com/research/

B.R.A.V.E. leaders know who they are, understand the power of compassion, are able to sit in empathy, and cultivate cultures of belonging everywhere they show up. THIS is the foundation for everything that B.R.A.V.E. Human Leadership is and these are the five words I chose that make up the acronym: Belonging, Resilience, Authenticity, Vulnerability, and Empathy.

The journey towards B.R.A.V.E. leadership might require unlearning some traditional notions about professional distance and command-style management. This is the Constrained Leader who believes that a strong leader needs to:

- Maintain authority over others to be effective.
- Be willing to make people uncomfortable to ensure good outcomes for the organization.
- Use psychological tricks to get the people they lead to do what they want them to do.
- Scare the people they lead so they'll work harder.[3]

On the other hand, the B.R.A.V.E. Human Leadership pathway advocates for a closer connection with your team members, acknowledging their individual strengths, struggles, and aspirations, which are often masked in purely results-focused interactions. Leaders who embrace these principles find themselves better equipped to handle the complexities of modern-day leadership where emotional intelligence plays as significant a role as strategic thinking. In fact, our research suggests that 57% of leaders strongly agreed that a leader should be the most emotionally intelligent person in the room. Through this section's exploration into diverse interpretations and applications of B.R.A.V.E., it is my hope that you will not only understand these principles but also learn how they can be practically applied to meet contemporary challenges head-on.[4]

The top challenges leaders today are facing are mostly about people: managing difficult people (36%), having enough time for responsibilities (32%), and letting employees go/firing people (31%). Relational Leaders are significantly more likely to struggle with firing people, and Constrained Leaders just can't quite figure out how to influence people.[5] Thus, embarking on this journey doesn't just mean adopting a new set of principles; it involves transforming into a leader who is ready for the future—one who leads not just with their mind but also with their heart in this age of digital disconnection. Moreso today than ever, we know the only way to lead forward from here successfully is to lead with B.R.A.V.E. intent.

*"The true mark of a leader is the willingness to stick with a bold course of action — an unconventional business strategy, a unique product-development roadmap, a controversial marketing campaign — even as the rest of the world wonders why you're not marching in step with the status quo. In other words, real leaders are happy to zig while others zag. They understand that in an era of hyper-competition and non-stop disruption, the only way to stand out from the crowd is to stand for something special."*[6]

*Bill Taylor, Fast Company co-founder*

## CHAPTER 9

# Belonging

Looking back on my stint in Little League Baseball, I can remember what it felt like to not belong. The feeling wasn't bigger than me when I was seven, and for all intents and purposes, my teammates, the other coaches and my own coach (aka Dad) made me feel like I was good enough to be there. The first time I ever even thought about the fact that I was a girl and I was playing ball in a sea of boys was the time I remember hearing a catcher on the other team unsure if he should block the plate when I hit a ball that kept rolling through the outfield as I was rounding third on my way home. My first instinct was, "Why are you even asking this? Because I am about to take you out." I mean, I wasn't going to go easy on him just because he was a boy.

The second moment was the "cup story" that I shared earlier in the book. Two questions from two different people who happened to be male were the only things that stopped me long enough to think that I was playing a "male sport."

That realization hit me a lot later in life. I was challenged back then by two people, who seemingly were asking honest questions they felt were required regarding nothing other than my gender. They were questions for *them* to handle the fact that I wasn't a boy and how to cope this fact. All of the rules, the framework, the constructs that our society has built told them this game was not for someone like me. What I have since realized is this asking comes in many different forms. Challenging people who are outside of the constructs built to exclude them in various ways, are based on the need for some to answer these types of questions:

**"What do I need to do differently because you don't represent what we have gotten used to fitting inside this box we built?"**

Or oftentimes,

**"Why do I need to make room for you because if I give you this space, there isn't room for me. And … this isn't your space anyway?"**

We can get really good at "othering" and sometimes, don't even realize we are doing it. This is the EXACT opposite of belonging and can feel awful for everyone involved, especially the one who is the recipient of the actions and words. Adding to this complexity is the phenomenon known as "context collapse," where diverse social groups converge in a single digital space. This can lead individuals to communicate in ways that are overly curated or generic, further diluting the authenticity of interactions and can result in conversations that are transactional rather than transformational, lacking the richness that comes from prolonged, meaningful discussions.

*Could understanding these limitations be the key to transforming our digital interactions into opportunities for genuine connection?*

When I was five, I had a Fisher-Price toy vacuum that made a lot of noise. Being the youngest of five kids, plus my parents, made for a noisy house of people jockeying for position when it came to airtime and attention. I remember vividly one Saturday afternoon my parents called a "family meeting." Not sure what that actually meant then, and perhaps even now, however they all came into the room together to discuss chores, house rules, family budgeting, or something that really didn't pertain to me at the time. Everyone was talking—some more than others and some over others. I remember sitting off to the side feeling totally left out of this "meeting." I got up, grabbed my little, yet very noisy vacuum, and dragged it into the center of the room where I proceeded to move it back and forth as hard as I could in order to make as much noise as possible. I wanted to be a part of the group, of the conversation. Even if I had nothing to say or no contribution to make in the situation, I wanted to feel seen and listened to. I just wanted to belong. I still do. We all do.

Taking a look back in your lifetime, I am quite sure you can think of a time where you felt like you didn't belong. I'm sure we can all agree that there's a certain anxiety that goes along with that feeling—times that you felt maybe you weren't a part of the conversation. You felt left out. You felt excluded in decision-making. How that shows up in the workplace is very consequential in so many different ways, some of which involve leadership, some of which involve engagement. Both hold an importance we can't overlook.

Think about some of those moments where maybe you saw someone around you going through this worrying stage, stressed that they do not belong in the workplace. Think about the toll that takes. This feeling highlights the importance of starting a conversation about exclusion. What does the act of being excluded in the workplace look like and how much does it detract from the work that we do? It shows up in a few different ways, one of which is being studied by psychologists around the globe and is being considered a real epidemic. Since COVID-19, the gap has only widened. It can be attributed to something that is so telling about how we are showing up in the workplace and beyond:

### *The disconnection of loneliness*

The damage loneliness does to the physical body is astounding. It also has very little to do with what's going on around you. I know I've had this feeling of sitting in a room of 50 people and feeling like I was completely alone. Being alone and being lonely are two different things. Just because I am surrounded by 50 other people, does not I am physically "alone" however, it may not eradicate the feeling of loneliness. Loneliness is about the internal feelings related to your state of mind and what you're going through, not about the amount of people around you. The most interesting part of all of this is that neuroscience research has shown us that the pain of exclusion and the perception of physical pain are both seen in the same networks in the brain.[1]

Research has also shown that when we are connected with others within a community, the sensory parts of the brain light up and neurons fire in unison with another.[2] This means that when we are in agreement with others or are connecting with them based on a certain topic or feeling, our brains exhibit something called neural coupling or synchrony.[3] This neural coupling is how our brains evolved and we from an evolutionary perspective, humans by default seek out opportunities to build communities with others. This is why our first instinct when we are in a new group of people is to seek out others who have similar interests to us. In addition, it is why, when we disagree on things or are in conflict with someone else, we tend to feel fatigued and overwhelmed. This is called cognitive disharmony, and it is why we tend to avoid conflict.[4] The brain is a lot more active during these times when looking for ways to connect. It makes sense that we are constantly looking to lighten the cognitive load in our brains just like we do from our schedules, tasks and things we physically carry. We don't want to hold onto them forever; it's too tiring.

The latest research also tells us that this loneliness doesn't only apply in social settings and within familial contexts. There is an increasing number of people in the workplace who have felt increasingly excluded and isolated in recent times than ever before. What is driving this and, more importantly, what can we do about it? The truth is, loneliness had been labeled an epidemic long before we were asked to isolate in the midst of a global pandemic. We have been trending in this direction for years. Now, it's just been highlighted because we could take a step back to look at it.[5]

Amy Edmondson is best known for researching the phenomenon known today as psychological safety. Her research suggests that without psychological safety, there can be no vulnerability or trust. This safety net keeps us living and connecting at the surface, never really allowing us to dive deeper into knowing each other or letting others know you. This lack of safe spaces creates more disconnect, covering, and hiding thus perpetuating loneliness.[6] The really scary results that emerged from this study is that the highest number, the age group that's at the greatest risk factor for reporting chronic loneliness, is 16- to 24-year-olds. This number is on the rise.[7]

We are in this space of trying to figure out how *we*, as a society, can begin to turn our attention to loneliness as an issue and begin to take action to mitigate this mental health epidemic. Mental health surveys that have been conducted indicate that teens are struggling with depression and anxiety at alarming rates. More broadly, more and more people struggle to stay afloat in every way tell us this is a topic we MUST be talking about.

***Every human being, every single one of us, wants two things in life: We want to be seen and we want to be listened to because that validates***

***our very human existence.*** These two desires are what reminds us that we are always enough. What is extremely apparent, however, is this validation of our worth and value, for some, is critically missing. How can we foster that feeling of inclusion and belonging to those around us? The answer is in understanding the power of belonging. How does this affect us in the workplace?

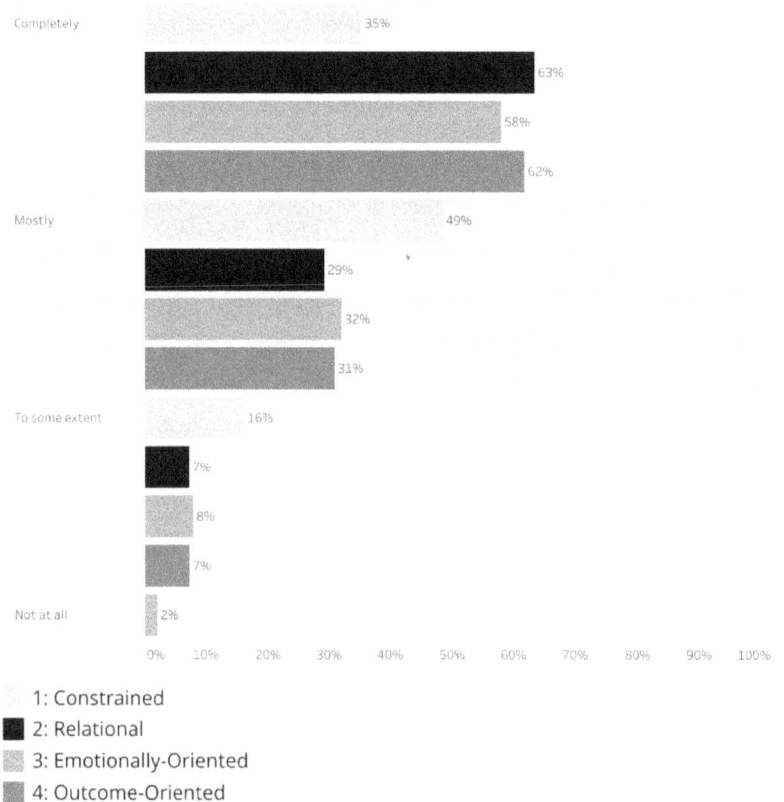

Figure 9.1: Organizations Cultivate Belonging

| Level | 1: Constrained | 2: Relational | 3: Emotionally-Oriented | 4: Outcome-Oriented |
|---|---|---|---|---|
| Completely | 35% | 63% | 58% | 62% |
| Mostly | 49% | 29% | 32% | 31% |
| To some extent | 16% | 7% | 8% | 7% |
| Not at all | 2% | | | |

- 1: Constrained
- 2: Relational
- 3: Emotionally-Oriented
- 4: Outcome-Oriented

Note: Q32 Belonging in the workplace means everyone can show up as their authentic selves. They feel accepted, supported, connected, and included. Organizations that create a sense of belonging embrace what is unique about each team member and encourage them to maintain that uniqueness. Do you feel your organization cultivates belonging? Audience Audit, & Human Leadership Institute. (2024, September). How

B.R.A.V.E. Human Leadership Behaviors Define Relational Leaders: Leading With Mind and Heart. https://www.thehli.com/research/

More than one in two Empathic Leaders (58%) from our research reported that their organizations completely cultivate belonging. However, nearly two in three (63%) of Relational Leaders also make this claim. On the other hand, only one-third (35%) of Constrained Leaders reported that their organizations completely cultivate belonging. Based on these differences across leader profiles, we wanted to take a look at why these results emerged.[8]

A December 2019 article in the *Harvard Business Review* says that 40% of people they surveyed said they felt isolated at work.[9] This number has climbed even higher over the past few years, due to the COVID-19 pandemic, during which we were asked to self-isolate and socially distance ourselves.[10] What's so astonishing is that the Harvard article was written right before the outbreak of the pandemic. Little did we know our lives and entire social paradigm would change so drastically just a few weeks later.

Organizations that don't understand the importance of B.R.A.V.E. Human Leadership are struggling to get creating a culture of belonging right. Businesses spend nearly eight **billion** dollars each year on DEI trainings[11] that don't deliver what is truly needed because:

*They neglect our desire to feel included in the process AND the outcome.*

The feeling of inclusion has not entered the workplace discourse as much as it should. At the end of the day, it is always about taking care of our people. How we deliver as leaders is what creates this culture effectively or not. It's not just a word: it's a set of behaviors that lead to a specific outcome and a specific feeling. It's rooted in the structures that hold those behaviors in place.

Regardless of all the good it does for the people of an organization, it's also safe to say that belonging is just flat out good for business. A 2019 study in The Harvard Business Review, found that belonging was linked to a 56% increase in job performance, a 50% decrease turnover rate, a 75% reduction in sick days and, overall, the feeling of inclusion and belonging is proven to cause employees to give more effort.[12]

How does this translate to numbers? For a 10,000-person company, this would result in a savings of more than $52 million a year.[13] The bottom line is that creating cultures of belonging in the workplace not only have a positive human impact, but also a positive economic impact. Right now, there are many businesses looking for ways to create a culture of belonging that is cost-effective. Leaders from our research already see the correlation: 57% believe strong leadership can boost productivity and improve morale. Relational Leaders are significantly more likely than Constrained Leaders to see these benefits (76% compared to 41%).[14]

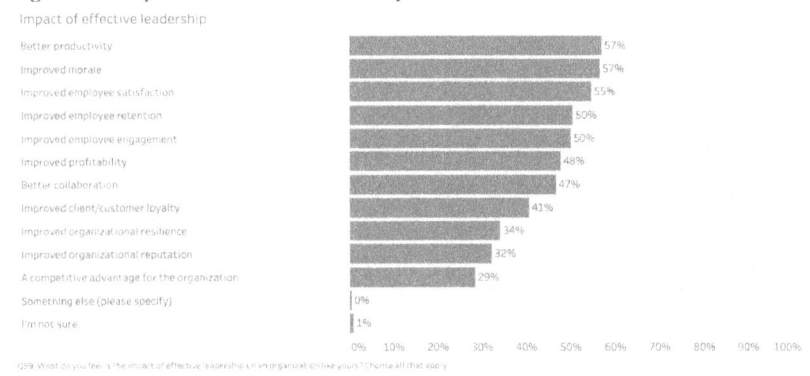

Figure 9.2: Impact of Effective Leadership

| Impact of effective leadership | |
|---|---|
| Better productivity | 57% |
| Improved morale | 57% |
| Improved employee satisfaction | 55% |
| Improved employee retention | 50% |
| Improved employee engagement | 50% |
| Improved profitability | 48% |
| Better collaboration | 47% |
| Improved client/customer loyalty | 41% |
| Improved organizational resilience | 34% |
| Improved organizational reputation | 32% |
| A competitive advantage for the organization | 29% |
| Something else (please specify) | 0% |
| I'm not sure | 1% |

Note: Q59 What do you feel is the impact of effective leadership on an organization like yours? Choose all that apply. Audience Audit, & Human Leadership Institute. (2024, September). How B.R.A.V.E. Human Leadership Behaviors Define Relational Leaders: Leading With Mind and Heart. https://www.thehli.com/research/

Figure 9.3: Impact of Effective Leadership By Segment

## Meet Them Where They Are

**Impact of effective leadership**

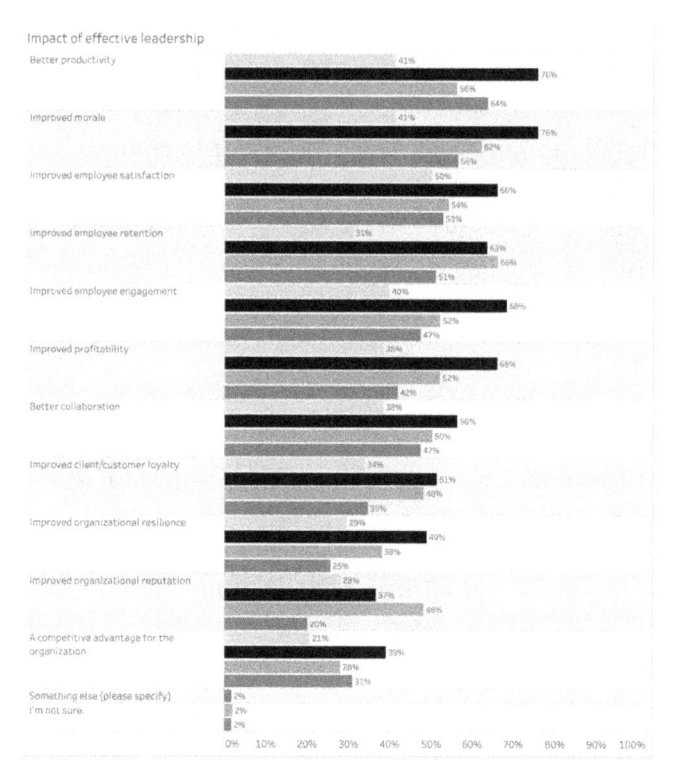

|  |  |
|---|---|
| Better productivity | 41%, 76%, 56%, 64% |
| Improved morale | 41%, 76%, 62%, 60% |
| Improved employee satisfaction | 50%, 66%, 54%, 53% |
| Improved employee retention | 31%, 63%, 66%, 51% |
| Improved employee engagement | 40%, 68%, 52%, 47% |
| Improved profitability | 38%, 68%, 52%, 42% |
| Better collaboration | 38%, 56%, 50%, 47% |
| Improved client/customer loyalty | 34%, 61%, 40%, 35% |
| Improved organizational resilience | 29%, 49%, 38%, 25% |
| Improved organizational reputation | 28%, 37%, 46%, 20% |
| A competitive advantage for the organization | 21%, 39%, 28%, 31% |
| Something else (please specify) | 2%, 2%, 2% |
| I'm not sure. | — |

Note: Q59 What do you feel is the impact of effective leadership on an organization like yours? Choose all that apply. Audience Audit, & Human Leadership Institute. (2024, September). How B.R.A.V.E. Human Leadership Behaviors Define Relational Leaders: Leading With Mind and Heart. https://www.thehli.com/research/

What does belonging look like in an organization? For more than half the leaders we asked, it's recognizing each other's accomplishments and creating a safe space where everybody can express opinions freely. Relational Leaders were more likely to cite various behaviors as foundational to creating a sense of belonging. These leaders are two times more likely to cite these certain behaviors than Constrained Leaders.[15]

101

B.R.A.V.E. Leaders know what an inclusive culture looks and more importantly feels like. They know that diversity is not enough and that checking boxes and counting seats at the table doesn't mean inclusion. They know that when they move the needle, they can create a *climate and culture* that isn't just focused on making inclusion something to talk about or a nice idea in theory. By pushing past boundaries and biases, B.R.A.V.E. Leaders lay a pathway to belonging that is a *permanent* way of doing business. Creating a culture of belonging is far more than performing a task, meeting a goal, or achieving a metric.

*It's a feeling.*
*It's a connectedness.*
*It's a purpose.*
*It's why your employees work for you and not someone else.*

Belonging, the marker beyond inclusion, becomes the cultural behavioral standard NOW, not just something to strive for in the future. Leading people is more than just making sure they do their jobs or meet their numbers—and it certainly is more than just a title.

What B.R.A.V.E. Leaders do differently is also centered in learning effective perspective taking. I talk a lot about belief windows, the idea of shared experience and understanding, and seeing from another's point of view. B.R.A.V.E. Leaders have to consider a variety of truths.

These belief windows are the lenses that we all look through and are what shape our world views. Think about some of the things that you see based on where you come from, based on where you grew up, based on your family structure. We all have different experiences about things. Naturally, we see things differently because we are looking at them from different perspectives. This means that we cannot experience the world exactly as another person because each person has different lived experiences. As leaders, it is important that we remember this when creating a culture of belonging. I believe we can really work hard

## Meet Them Where They Are

at perspective-taking and understanding that these belief windows don't need to get in the way—they can actually help us. I call this #cometouchmysideoftheelephant.

When I was younger, my dad shared with me the old Indian tale of the three men and the elephant. It goes something like this ... Pretend you've never seen an elephant before. Three blindfolded individuals are going to explain an elephant to you over the telephone. All they have is their ability to touch, so they're going to explain to you what they're feeling.

The first person is standing at the tail of the elephant and says, "Okay, so I'm here, I'm touching this elephant thing and it feels like a rope."

You say, "Rope? I know what a rope is. I must now know what an elephant is. Thank you very much, have a good day."

The second person is standing at the tusk of the elephant and says, "I'm not sure why the first person is leading you astray. I heard what they said and they aren't right. I'm standing at the elephant and it feels like a lead pipe. It's solid. I am touching it, so I know it's true."

Now you're saying, "Hmmm ... rope, lead pipe? Two totally different things, right? Get on the same page you two!"

The third person is standing at the leg of the elephant and says, "I have no idea what's happening here, but I'm going to tell you. I'm standing here, I'm at the elephant and it actually feels big, round, and rough, like a tree trunk." Now you just hang up the phone because you're confused, you're annoyed, and you're frustrated.

Although each person is seemingly describing a different object, they are all accurately describing parts of an elephant that their limited and constrained experiences permit. Because they cannot see and explore the entire elephant, their descriptions are vastly different and inaccurately describe the entire picture. I think today, more than ever, we need more #cometouchmysideoftheelephant moments. This means we walk with someone else for a moment in time to listen, see, and understand by facing the same way and looking in the same direction. Then, when we're finished, we're going to turn the other way and we're going to look at it from that direction. The more we do that, the more opportunity to listen to other's experiences, the more opportunity to be able to be a really good perspective-taker. We are much better able to stand in someone else's shoes if we actually put them on first. That is what has always been taught about how to show up in the world creating a space for others to feel seen:

### *Stand in their shoes.*

It sounds great in theory. The challenge comes when you realize that there is no way to ever really do it. I truly believe we will NEVER actually be able to be fully immersed in someone else's world and see exactly what they do. What we CAN do is we can seek to understand it, feel it, and know it in even the smallest of ways.

### *The humanness is relatable if we allow it to be*

Let us take grief, for example. Grief is a feeling that we have all experienced in our own way. While we will never have the exact experiences, we *are* able to recognize grief in others because of the human element we all share: what grief FEELS like. We have all grieved for someone, something, or some element of our lives that is no longer present. The circumstances and causes are unique, but the feeling is universal.

This is one reason that we created the B.R.A.V.E. Human Leadership model: to help us better relate to others. It's about being able to sit in the midst of someone else's experience and allow yourself to know what you don't know and to listen with an open heart based on the universal truth that we ALL believe to be true in some way. That we are best as people, as leaders, and as organizations when we stop to make sure that this B.R.A.V.E. framework is not just understood, but enacted across communities of people so they FEEL, not just hear. It is not enough that we talk about it, but that we seek out ways to build collaboration and innovation. This doesn't happen unless it is properly laid in the hands of trust and psychological safety. It is paramount in those moments to identify ways to take action and initiative and to find ways to help other people do the same.

Belonging is more than just fitting in. Perhaps, it may be just the opposite. Fitting in is working to assimilate: to bend and mold yourself to fit the group's norms regardless of how much authenticity you lose in the process. Belonging is actually being authentically you, regardless of how different you may be to others in the group. Belonging is the feeling we have when we stand in the midst of the place we love the most (e.g., the beach, the edge of a lake, or in the middle of Central Park) and feel completely connected to your inner self and at peace, or at home.

There's this idea about belonging that I love the most and have heard a few times now from other colleagues, one of whom was at a retreat with Author and Podcast Host, Glennon Doyle. When you get a group of people together and you stand in a circle, maybe at a social gathering or in the office, instead of standing in a circle, stand in the shape of a horseshoe.[16] Always leave that end open for someone to be invited in. Think about it. If you're an introvert or not someone who would just interject yourself into a circle of people in conversation, you probably won't just walk up and shove your way in. There's never really a good way to stick yourself in there, is there? But if you're in a horseshoe, you always leave a space to invite people in and they won't feel as uncomfortable walking up and wanting to be a part of it.

This is one little inclusive behavior that we can take action on to help foster belonging.

As a leader, you can add to this list every day, and I encourage you to do so. However, one surefire way to make sure you all find the same page at some point is to focus your efforts on solidifying your vision, mission, and purpose. When we are looking for a strong sense of belonging, find the ways that people can connect and relate to each other as well as to the core values of the company. This is what we center our very own human story around. Getting good at telling that story is everything.

On March 4th, 2020, *Forbes* published an article that I wrote about getting clear on your vision, mission, and purpose and understanding the difference and the importance of each.[17] Of course, I'm not a fortune teller by any means. Nobody, including me, had any idea that nine days later here in the United States, we would be going through a massive shutdown like nothing we have ever lived through before. What I know for sure, leaning on those three principles, is that I'm seeing the pendulum swing back to the human being, instead of always talking about the where and the what. We're talking more about the who and the why, because again, at the end of the day it's always about how we want to feel. Good companies recognize the fact that PEOPLE will always be their greatest asset. Recognizing that human beings will ALWAYS, at the end of the day, be the differential that makes the company move and grow and thrive.

This conversation is more important than ever. Right now B.R.A.V.E. Leaders need to know how to paint these visions of creating a culture of belonging that will be as strong as their people. When we open the dialogue to understanding instead of just listening, and actually inviting others in instead of just staying in the same place, we open ourselves to this beautiful space of belonging. ***Come, join us. You belong here!***

## CHAPTER 10

# Resilience

Resilience is described in the context of how we recover after a mistake or failure. It's what we have lived through these past few years as a human race. It's practicing humanity in crisis. B.R.A.V.E. Leaders do exactly this. They don't leave anyone behind, regardless of what they're going through. They're able to reach out and make sure that they take care of ALL of their people.

Resilience is about advancing despite adversity. It's about adapting despite of what surrounds us. It's knowing how to create a path forward, regardless of where we find ourselves in any given moment. I see it as being able to take the shape to fit the edges that are given to us, and sometimes the edges that are given to us can be difficult to expand into. Nevertheless, being able to have this adaptability is important. In the sports psychology world, we talked a lot about flow amidst chaos. Flow is a concept that has been incredibly intriguing to me over my career. We often studied the intricacies and energy of flow. Some people call it "being in the zone."

One expert on this topic is Dr. Mihalyi Chzysentmihalyi and in studying his work, I started to really understand how the mind and body are connected.[1] Flow means: Being resilient in the midst of chaos, no matter what is going on around us. Being focused and in control of our thoughts that we are lost in the midst of whatever we're doing or mastering. Flow is almost like getting lost in time and space. Time stands still and you don't even recognize what's going on around you. Flow amidst chaos is really what mastering resilience is about. It's the ability to make decisions and act quickly. It's staying optimistic and taking others with you to teach them to do the same.

Do you remember the process of learning how to walk? Think back for a second. I'm sure you probably don't remember actually learning how to walk because neither do I. We were obviously very young when we did that, but try to think about it, nevertheless. Even if you don't remember it yourself, I'm sure you've seen someone learn how to walk, right? What does it look like? The first couple of steps are unsure … you know: very wobbly and very insecure. Children fall down, and then they get back up and do it again. This repeats over and over until what? Until they master it.

This actually tells me one really important thing. Your ability to fall down and get back up is innate. You're born with that. Humans have been developing resilience since before we could form memories. It is a part of who we are and we need to continue to develop this innate since of resilience throughout our entire lifetimes. Sometimes we're really good at it and other times we falter. Think about where resilience shows up in your current life's journey. What does it look like for us on a day-to-day basis of working through a crisis, really seeing this idea of flow amidst chaos play out? Does it emerge when you are at your best? Can you show your people what that looks like? Can you teach others to do the same? Can you get up after you have fallen … yet, again?

I believe resilience is the gift we get from adversity. It's like giving us the chance to start over or to rewrite the part of the story we didn't like. It is really a choice in how we see it. We can view our situation as grim, dark, and terrible or we can have a change in perspective and frame things as optimistic and full of possibility. The possibility of everything around us, to me, is what gives me hope every single day. It's what makes me want to get up and do this work, especially when it's hard. *We* choose how we see just about everything. As we can't change the things that happen to us that we have no control over, we can only choose how we respond, every single time.

## WHAT OUR RESEARCH HAS SHOWN:

**46% of leaders say their organizations completely cultivate resilience. Relational Leaders set the average, with 46% saying resilience is the norm at their organizations. In this case, two-in-three Outcome-Oriented Leaders say resilience is the status quo at their organizations, making them the most likely of all segments to be succeeding in this regard.**[2]

**And so where does this leave us? How can we keep flexing the resilience muscle, sometimes daily, when our bodies and minds are beyond tired?**

I have a Monday story for you. I call it the Monday Principle.

I was in the grocery store on a Monday at 11:00 AM. If you've ever been in a grocery store on a Monday morning, pre -COVID, you know there's not much happening. It was typically me, the retired folk, the stay-at-home moms and dads, the work from home people, and a few stragglers who just didn't get there over the weekend. The big picture: not much is happening. I'm standing in the checkout line with the two things I needed in my hands. The woman in front of me, as it always happens, has an entire cart full of stuff. I'm waiting patiently and she proceeds to put her last item on the conveyor belt and gets her hand caught in the handle of her purse. And in a split second, dumps her purse all over the floor.

I'm looking down thinking to myself (I didn't say this out loud, but I certainly thought it), "*Lady, you need to clean out your purse because this is about to take us a half hour to clean up.*" I knelt down with her and immediately helped her pick up her things as everything is now scattered all over the floor. As I am handing her things to her, stuff is rolling into the next lane. She looks up at me and we are now face-to-face. She loudly sighs and follows it with these words in a sing-songy, frustrated tune:

"It's Mooondaaaay."

To which I replied, "Yep, it sure is. As a matter of fact, yesterday was Sunday. I know you're not going to believe this but tomorrow is Tuesday."

And I took a step back. I wasn't sure what was about to happen. She just looked up at me very quickly and shook her head in disgust and a let out a loud "UGH."

Now we're picking up her stuff in silence. "Here you go, here's this, here's that," I said as I was reaching for the last couple of things under the magazine rack. She turns to the cashier, she pays, and she puts her last bag in her cart. She's about to walk away and I thought, "*Yikes, I got away with one there.*" Then she stops. I thought to myself, "*Uh oh, here it comes.*"

She slowly turns around. It was like five minutes. I'm standing there waiting to see what was about to happen. I felt like I was in the movie The Matrix. She was totally in slow motion. Finally, I see her face. She has a huge smile on and she starts to laugh.

She looked at me and she said, "You know what, thank you for that."

I simply said, *"BAD MOMENTS, NOT BAD DAYS."*

That is a choice. Resilience actually can be a choice. We may not always have a choice in what happens, but we have a choice in how we see it and how we react to it. Make a decision, take action, and in the middle: "figure it out." We have search engines and articles and people to ask. We can figure anything out if we really want to. Resilience is a choice of whether we get back up or we bring a cozy blanket and a pillow and stay there on the floor for a while. Most days, I choose to get back up.

Jennifer Lynne Croneberger

# WHAT OUR RESEARCH HAS SHOWN:

Figure 10.1: What Resilience Looks Like By Leadership Segment

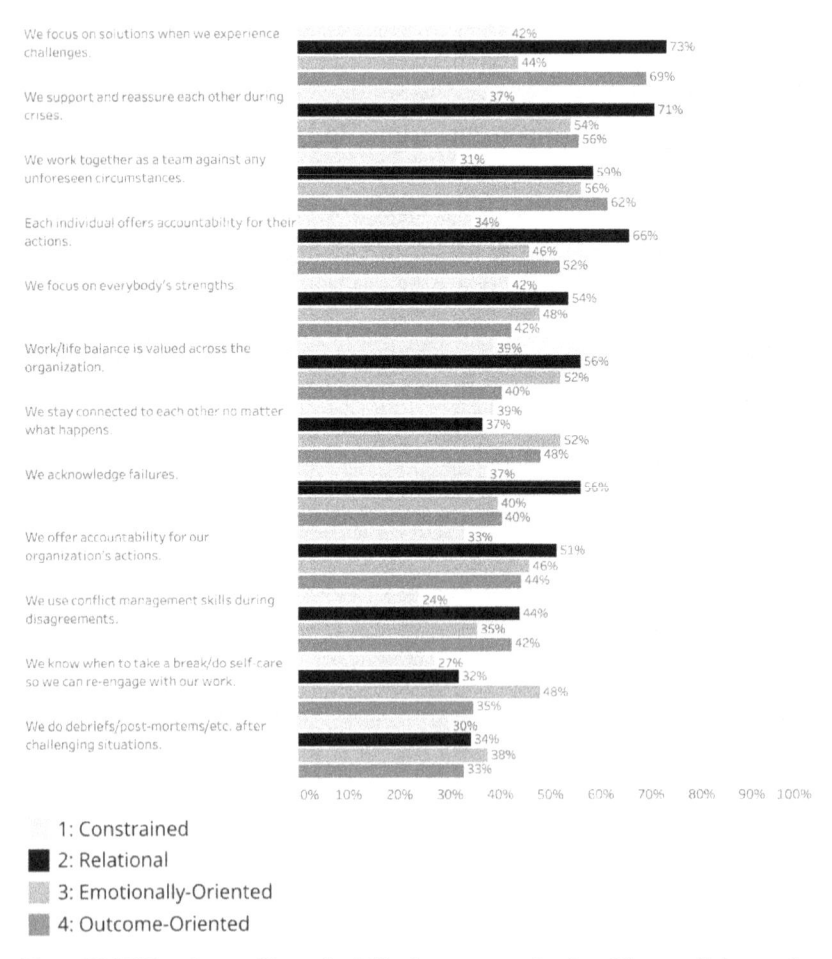

| Statement | Constrained | Relational | Emotionally-Oriented | Outcome-Oriented |
|---|---|---|---|---|
| We focus on solutions when we experience challenges. | 42% | 73% | 44% | 69% |
| We support and reassure each other during crises. | 37% | 71% | 54% | 56% |
| We work together as a team against any unforeseen circumstances. | 31% | 59% | 56% | 62% |
| Each individual offers accountability for their actions. | 34% | 66% | 46% | 52% |
| We focus on everybody's strengths. | 42% | 54% | 48% | 42% |
| Work/life balance is valued across the organization. | 39% | 56% | 52% | 40% |
| We stay connected to each other no matter what happens. | 39% | 37% | 52% | 48% |
| We acknowledge failures. | 37% | 56% | 40% | 40% |
| We offer accountability for our organization's actions. | 33% | 51% | 46% | 44% |
| We use conflict management skills during disagreements. | 24% | 44% | 35% | 42% |
| We know when to take a break/do self-care so we can re-engage with our work. | 27% | 32% | 48% | 35% |
| We do debriefs/post-mortems/etc. after challenging situations. | 30% | 34% | 38% | 33% |

1: Constrained
2: Relational
3: Emotionally-Oriented
4: Outcome-Oriented

Note: Q36 What does resilience look like in your organization. Choose all that apply. Audience Audit, & Human Leadership Institute. (2024, September). How B.R.A.V.E. Human Leadership Behaviors Define Relational Leaders: Leading With Mind and Heart. https://www.thehli.com/research/

**About one in two leaders cultivate resilience in their organization by focusing on solutions when there are challenges, supporting and reassuring each other during crises, and working together as a team against any unforeseen circumstances. Relational Leaders cite more ways their organizations demonstrate resilience. As with belonging, they're sometimes nearly twice as likely to note specific resilience behaviors compared to Constrained Leaders.**[3]

---

### CASE STUDY

Jackie Felicetti, Retired CHRO—Chester County Hospital, Penn Medicine

---

Perhaps one of the greatest unforeseen circumstances in our lifetime was COVID-19 and how it impacted every aspect of our lives in a matter of moments. Our healthcare system and the people that continued, day in and day out, to make it run were severely impacted. Regardless of the circumstances, they showed up and did whatever they were called upon to do.

Jackie and I started to work together in 2020, just after the murder of George Floyd and the continued swell of a global pandemic. That beginning conversation between us about how we could work together to build a stronger and more inclusive culture became a three-year-long relationship between Chester County Hospital and JLynne Consulting Group (JLCG)/The Human Leadership Institute (HLI). To say it was a trying time to be doing this work, in healthcare, is an understatement. Yet, through this incredible experience of really learning what it meant to serve others regardless of situation, I saw the rise of the human spirit in ways I had never seen before. The following is a conversation about resilience through the eyes of someone who witnessed it all from the ground floor.

*The following viewpoints expressed below are solely those of the individual and in no way represent the views or statements of Penn Medicine.

*Jen*: Jackie, thank you for taking this time to share your experiences and thoughts with us.

How long have you worked in healthcare?

*Jackie:* I have worked in healthcare for 33 years. I have always been in Human Resources so my main role was to provide support to the frontline healthcare workers as well as everyone else who helps to keep the lights on in the healthcare organization.

*Jen*: In those 33 years, have you ever experienced a tougher time than what you saw in the last few years? I would love for you to share your story from the inside. Tell us a little bit about what that was like.

*Jackie*: Working early on with COVID and trying to figure out what this Novel Coronavirus-19 was, and then trying to bring the organization back to some kind of normalcy in 2022 was challenging. I cannot say it was the absolute hardest time I saw in my career, at least not from my standpoint. I will get to that later. COVID made us, almost overnight, re-engineer everything we did. The virus impacted the work of every single employee, student, volunteer, contractor, board member, including the patients and the entire community. From learning how to be very judicious with our PPE (personal protective equipment), learning how to don and doff properly as not to contaminate oneself, to learn how to have patients visit their loved ones virtually, staff learning to work from home, dealing with emotions and stress of staff who were seeing patients die like they had never seen before. Even staff having to worry daily that they would bring this new unknown virus home to their families from the hospital. These are just some examples of the underlying picture of what this level of resilience was, or needed to be.

The organization and the people in it had to be resilient in order to survive mentally and financially, while keeping at the center their overall pursuit of providing quality care to the patients. I experienced a plethora of people leaving healthcare for fear of the virus and the fear of the new vaccine. Fear of the unknown can do damage to a person's psyche.

What I quickly learned was that the resiliency of healthcare workers amazed me. I saw people picking up extra shifts during COVID because of being short staffed. This happened often because many workers had to be out of work due to exposure at work, at home, or in the community. Some contracted the virus themselves. I experienced staff wanting to cross-train into other roles, temporarily, to help during these staffing shortages. I witnessed an administrative professional (non-bedside) learn to don and doff properly to teach others to not contaminate themselves. I saw a well-seasoned professional work tirelessly to take care of all her patients even though she recently had lost her brother to COVID.

I witnessed silos breaking down. It was no longer viewed as "this is my department, this is your department", it became one big department. It truly became the department of patient care.

I watched daily as our CEO covered himself head to toe in PPE and visited staff and patients in all units including floors that had mostly COVID patients. I was amazed by this because so many others would be too afraid to be contaminated if they didn't need to be. We knew the virus was highly contagious and the fact that it affected everyone differently was like a roll of the dice. In my mind, he reminded me of a descendant of Mother Teresa. A true leader who wasn't afraid to lead his people. That was a picture for all of us of what resiliency really looked like.

One of our favorite doctors went to one of our sister hospitals that was hit incredibly hard and over-run with COVID patients. The fact that he went the extra mile to not just take care of his own staff and pressures here, but to go there to pitch in and help like they were his own was real resilience.

I saw front line staff stay at a hotel that the organization paid for as they did not want to take any potential virus home to their families. Some had newborn babies or a spouse with cancer and needed to take precautions to not infect them. One front-line staff member slept in his garage to avoid going into the house and potentially impacting the welfare of his family. Before vaccines or other therapeutics were introduced, it was all we could do to at least just mitigate the spread.

Getting back to what we would consider "normalcy" in my opinion was very hard. There were so many unanswered questions and the need for directives on the fly. Things like "when do we take down plexiglass, how long do we allow staff to still work at home, when do we change our policies back from restrictions during COVID?" Administratively, that was challenging.

Besides a global pandemic, there certainly have been other additional challenging times. Healthcare has been under significant financial pressures for a while. Things like reimbursements being cut, the increase in the cost of supplies, insurances and wage increases, etc. Merging with another organization (although incredibly helpful, and badly needed), was of course a challenge in and of itself as it would be any time. With that would be tremendous challenges to make sure it would be as seamless as possible. Not the same kinds of pressures on the system we saw with COVID, but certainly the merger was hard for many.

As with any merger, there are always questions surrounding which organization was more efficient with certain aspects of the business? The constant worry of whether or not we would lose our nimbleness and all of our sovereignty and power over localized decisions, etc. Processes like adopting several new computer systems and programs in a very short period of time created a ton of angst and concern.

Still, because the merger was for the greater good and we were very lucky to be a part of this incredibly prestigious academic organization, we had to power through and demonstrate resilience. Instead of people fearing change, the philosophy became to embrace it all. Embrace the new computer systems and process changes, the entirety of change and newness. That new resilience became a part of who we were at the core.

The hardest part for me?

It wasn't so much being positive, supportive, and engaged. Whatever we were dealt with was what we needed to do and I embraced that part. The hardest part for me was keeping up with the ever-changing policies, new info from CMS (Centers for Medicare & Medicaid Services), COVID benefits that impacted employees, COVID resource hours, visitor policy changes, the ambiguity surrounding how a person became exposed, etc. We needed to be a resource and we were, but in doing so, we needed to learn how to stay nimble, flexible, and positive in the midst of constant change. This was possibly one of the greatest challenges we faced. It still wasn't the hardest.

The hardest part of my employment in the last five years was the passing of George Floyd and the impact it had on everyone in our workplace. Resilience, understanding, and the social impact that event, among others like it, carried throughout the hospital was something I never expected to experience. There was a whole lot of learning, both positive and negative. And through that, we learned a lot about our own humanness. It was an important time for us to reflect on the power of inclusion and really diving into creating a culture where everyone felt they belonged. We wanted the hospital to be a safe space for ALL. It was our intent to make sure that was the case and we worked hard to build safe spaces and open lines of communication.

Now, in retirement, I have to be resilient. I am learning to live another kind of life. I moved from my home, left my job, have new surroundings, new grocery stores, etc. Through this process, however, I am slowing down enough to realize and live the beauty in the everyday moments. I am committing to embarking on learning new things, and my own new growth to find my way from here. I am grateful to have had all of those years in a career and with people I loved and cared for deeply.

Resilience is more than just getting up after we fall or recovering after a mistake. For someone like Jackie, it is truly a leadership behavior that has lasting implications toward the beautiful legacy she left behind in retirement. May we all strive to help each other get back up.

# CHAPTER 11

# Authenticity

Followers love leaders they can trust. That's a no-brainer. Trust is everything and we can't have it unless we know we are in a safe and genuine relationship. We all know an Authentic Leader. Those are the people you just want to be around. When you think about people who embody that authenticity, what is the one quality? How did you know that they were authentic? What made them authentic and trustworthy? What did that look like? Were they consistent, sincere, honest, personal, open, humble, willing to admit mistakes, and wanting to be the best version of themselves? All of those different traits make up exactly who we want to be as a leader. As B.R.A.V.E. Leaders, we have to understand the balance behind being and doing. Authenticity is a foundation on which we invite others to show up the same way following our leadership example as the true north.

WHAT OUR RESEARCH HAS SHOWN:

**Over one in two leaders say their organizations completely cultivate authenticity.**

**Once again, about one in two Relational Leaders say this is the case at their organizations. It's the Outcome-Oriented Leaders that head up the pack, with two in three saying authenticity is table stakes at their organizations.**[1]

Why is it then that we show some of our true selves and often hold back the rest? Let's go beneath the surface to the innermost aspects of ourselves that most people don't see or we don't let see. I want you to think about why. Think about what we show and what we hold back. Are there places where you're not being as authentic as you could be? Are there situations where you could really roll up your sleeves and say, "You know what? Here, I'm going to show up as myself, as my BEST self and the rest doesn't matter?" Are you willing to do that because you know that showing up that way is the willingness to be an authentic, B.R.A.V.E. Leader?

If not … what holds you back?

Authentic leaders are self-aware and genuine. They focus on long-term vision, are mission and purpose driven, and lead with their heart. I call this the L.I.G.H.T. principle, which stands for: love, integrity, gratitude, humor, and truth. This is always my check-in. I find it has been such an important process for me to develop myself as a leader. Have a check-in for yourself. Are you showing up the way you want to be showing up in the world? You don't have to use this specific mantra, but if you want to, I am happy to have shared it with you. When I show up this way, utilizing those principles, I am showing up as a B.R.A.V.E. Leader. I am showing up as my best, most authentic self: the "me" who I want to bring to the people I serve.

What then keeps that authenticity rooted in place? What holds onto the importance of authentic leadership? This was interesting to me so I did a little digging into this idea. The concept comes from Greek philosophy and focuses on the development of core values and virtues that create this foundation of an authentic leader.² I'm sure you've heard the phrase "know thyself" and in Greek the translation is: *gnōthi seauton*.

If you look back in history, those words were actually inscribed on the arch above the Temple of Apollo at Delphi. "Knowing thyself" was a huge tenant of Greek philosophy. If you didn't know yourself, you were not invited to enter the temple. Three virtues that were born out of this tenant of Greek philosophy are: prudence, temperance, and fortitude. This doesn't feel so far away from what we look for today in the leaders we choose to hire, learn from, and follow.³ That›s what makes the people around them better and that's what B.R.A.V.E. leaders must bring to the table every day.

Jennifer Lynne Croneberger

# WHAT OUR RESEARCH HAS SHOWN:

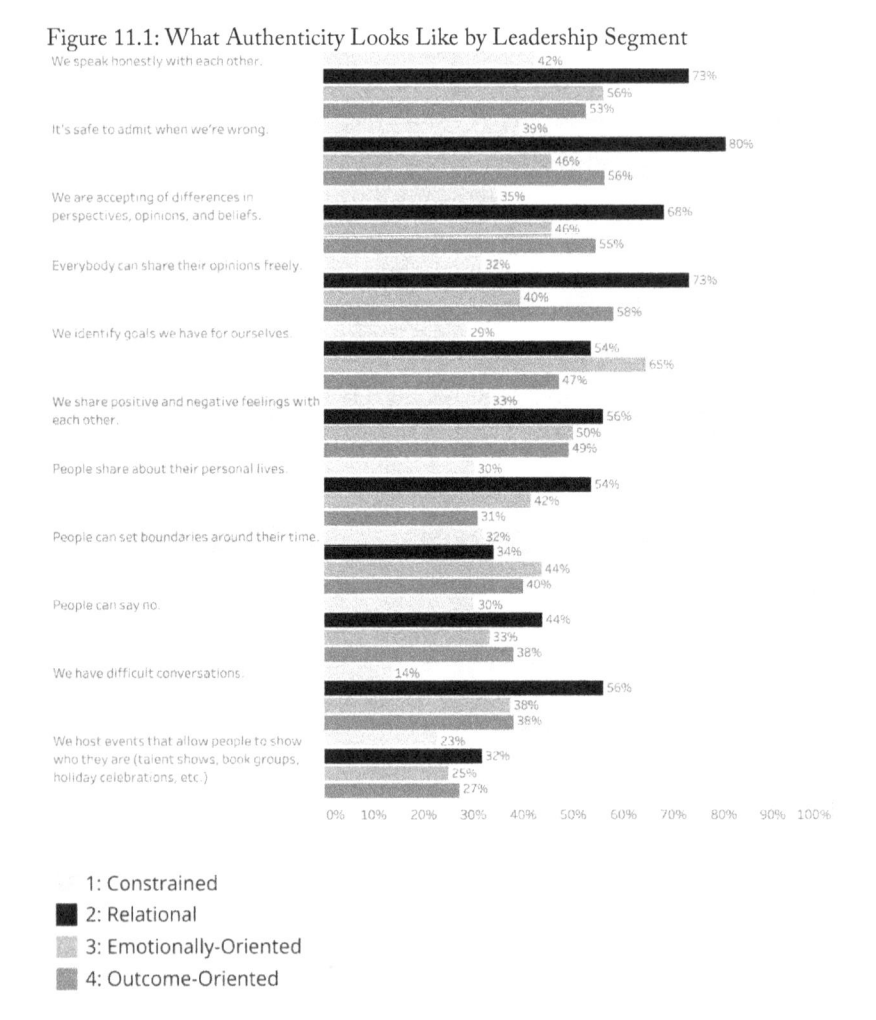

Figure 11.1: What Authenticity Looks Like by Leadership Segment

| Statement | 1: Constrained | 2: Relational | 3: Emotionally-Oriented | 4: Outcome-Oriented |
|---|---|---|---|---|
| We speak honestly with each other. | 42% | 73% | 56% | 53% |
| It's safe to admit when we're wrong. | 39% | 80% | 46% | 56% |
| We are accepting of differences in perspectives, opinions, and beliefs. | 35% | 68% | 46% | 55% |
| Everybody can share their opinions freely. | 32% | 73% | 40% | 58% |
| We identify goals we have for ourselves. | 29% | 54% | 65% | 47% |
| We share positive and negative feelings with each other. | 33% | 56% | 50% | 49% |
| People share about their personal lives. | 30% | 54% | 42% | 31% |
| People can set boundaries around their time. | 32% | 34% | 44% | 40% |
| People can say no. | 30% | 44% | 33% | 38% |
| We have difficult conversations. | 14% | 56% | 38% | 36% |
| We host events that allow people to show who they are (talent shows, book groups, holiday celebrations, etc.) | 23% | 32% | 25% | 27% |

- 1: Constrained
- 2: Relational
- 3: Emotionally-Oriented
- 4: Outcome-Oriented

Note: Q40 What does authenticity look like in your organization? Choose all that apply. Audience Audit, & Human Leadership Institute. (2024, September). How B.R.A.V.E. Human Leadership Behaviors Define Relational Leaders: Leading With Mind and Heart. https://www.thehli.com/research/

Our research shows that for one in two leaders, authenticity looks like speaking honestly with each other, safety to admit when they're wrong, and accepting of different perspectives, opinions, and beliefs. Relational Leaders are more likely to cite various expressions of authenticity. They're also significantly more likely than Constrained Leaders and, at times, Emotionally Oriented Leaders to speak honestly, safely admit when they're wrong, accept different ways of being, and share opinions freely, sometimes by 30-40 percentage points.[4]

---

### INTERVIEW/CASE STUDY

Tracy Davidson, NBC10 News Anchor-Philadelphia

---

Tracy Davidson is a 14-time Emmy Award-winning journalist, speaker, and thought-leader who focuses on resilience, authenticity, and sharing her inspiring story with those around her. I am lucky to also call her my friend and co-founder of Lifting Your Voice, a biannual event we host for women in our community to take a breath from everyday life, connect with other women, and step into their power.
I asked her about how she shows up in the world and the authenticity it takes to live in front of a camera:

*Jen*: As a journalist, how have you navigated authenticity to balance your career and personal life?

*Tracy:* People always say something like "you can only be yourself because everyone else is taken." But it's not that easy. In the UK, they call on-air journalists "presenters", which I guess is true. A TV journalist's job is really two parts: the journalist and the on-air presenter. When you're first starting out, consultants tell you how to position your hands, how to look at your co-anchor, how to look down between stories (even though there's no real need to do so). It all feels very unnatural and fake. You work so hard to emphasize the correct word in a sentence and not stumble in your "reads". On top of all that, they tell you to relax and be yourself. But they just told you to be a whole bunch of other things that you have to think about constantly.

As years go by you get more comfortable in what is a very foreign and unnatural space: the set, with its lights, moving cameras and teleprompter. Something else happens too. You get more comfortable with yourself in that space. The "rules" of how to behave on the set to be a good "anchor" start to fade or maybe they just become second nature. You begin to feel more confident in your own skin. You also begin to believe that if you're fully present while telling a story, it doesn't matter if you stumble over a word. Because that's how people talk. We are not perfect in how we relay a story. You begin to believe that "realness" is how to authentically communicate.

When you get decades into your career, you realize the value of that authenticity. When you ask about navigating in both career and personal life, I feel like a factor that has made it easier is that I had to decide early on in my career what I stood for—my priorities/my brand. And when you stand for something that is true to your core, it's easy to show up that way both professionally and personally.

*Jen*: Do you have someone in your career that has been a guide for how to do that effectively? Maybe a role model of authenticity early on in your work life?

*Tracy:* Early on in my career I had a role model: a woman who worked in an all-male newsroom (until I came along). She always seemed at ease with who she was and didn't have a hard time sharing that. But back then, she was still telling me, "As women, we have to work harder, do better, and look better doing it."

I think we get a lot of messages from the time we're young children about how we are supposed to "be", how we are to look (what clothes to wear, how long our hair should be, what "pretty" looks like), how we are to act (don't be loud, don't be bossy, don't show off), and who we are to hang out with; that our value is based on our looks, our studies, our athletic prowess, our talents. It's no wonder it takes a while to see/feel/know your authentic self … and then to have the confidence or even peace to share that with the world.

*Jen*: What does that professional balance look like?

*Tracy*: No doubt your authenticity should look different in the workplace than with your friends. But we should not underestimate how vulnerability and authenticity can serve us and those around us. So how much do you show/share? I liken it to advice a social media advisor gives to journalists about how much to share on social media. Obviously, as a journalist you want people to connect with you and trust you, so you want to share some things about who you are as a person. But there's a difference between "personal" and "private" and the journalist needs to decide where that line is.

In business, a person needs to decide what's personal and reasonable to share … that can strengthen relationships. One instance comes to mind. During a team review of a newscast, the executive producer (the one in charge) admitted that he made a mistake. He explained why he made a decision that turned out to be wrong and explained what he learned from it. Besides from the actual event, that showed everyone a lot about that person. He was authentic and vulnerable. No doubt your authenticity should look a little different in the workplace than with your friends, AND we should not underestimate how vulnerability and authenticity can serve us and those around us.

Many times in workshops and "Connective Coaching" sessions, I have asked a room full of executives a simple yet very complex question that caused a long conversation after the fact, often woven together with some laughter and some tears. The question is this:

*"Who are you?"*

The response usually is a long list of roles they play and titles they hold. It often is very superficial. A few years ago I was speaking at an event in New York and I was working with a room full of educators. I had delivered the keynote that morning and we were moving on to the breakout workshop later that afternoon. We got to talking about knowing who we were. I popped the question. After giving them some time to write their responses in their workbook, I asked for a few volunteers to share what they had written.

An older woman from the middle of the room raised her hand. She started to rattle them off …"I'm a wife, a mother, a grandmother, a friend, a sister and a special education teacher." I smiled and thanked her for sharing.

"Ok, who's next?" I asked, ready for someone else to volunteer.

A young woman in the front raised her hand and started to read her list, "I'm a daughter, a wife, a friend, a teacher, a child of God, a work in progress."

I smiled again. "Thank you," I said softly. Then the next, a middle-aged man who was excited to share he just became a dad. And one more.

Again, a list. I paused quietly for a second and then asked the next question, "So, I am going to challenge you here … is that WHO you are or is that WHAT you are?" … The room was quiet. I spoke again, "The list you gave me sounds like a list of roles you play for everyone in your life. What happens if you remove everyone else … then, can you tell me, who are you?" If the quiet could get quieter, it did. You could hear a pin drop. And then, I heard it. The quiet sniffling of the older woman in the middle of the room. The tears, rolling down her cheek.

"WOW … I didn't know I would get so emotional," she said. "I don't know how to answer that. I don't think I know who I am."

This same conversation has been repeated time and time again. Most of us define who we are based on the people we surround ourselves with, based on the roles we play in those places and situations, and for everyone but ourselves. Who we are at the core of us is deeper than that. It focuses more on our non-negotiables, the things we won't compromise for anyone. Defining who those are is a lot harder, and takes a lot of introspection. Sometimes it simply takes time.

We need to sit with that question in order to really have an anchor, a landing place when it all gets hard. This will always be your truth. So … let me ask you something:

*** WHO ARE YOU? ***
*Take your time.*
*You're worth it.*

**CHAPTER 12**

# Vulnerability

My first understanding of vulnerability was sitting next to my dad watching movies as a kid. There were two in particular that I remember. The first was *Chariots of Fire* (I can still hear the music in my head as I picture the men in white shorts and t-shirts running down the beach) and the second was *Mr. Holland's Opus.*

I grew up with a dad who very openly shed tears when he felt emotion. And not just when someone had died or something really sad happened. He would cry listening to the Hallelujah Chorus, Mandy Patinkin singing "Finishing the Hat" in *Sunday in the Park with George*, or anything that portrayed the vulnerability and thus the triumph of the human spirit. I saw it for one of the first times when I sat next to him to watch *Chariots of Fire* as a young girl. The audible crying and the tears that streamed down his face made me pause in wonder. I watched in the dark light of the living room as he cried. I asked him only once if he was ok. When he said yes and squeezed my hand the way he always did, I understood. I felt something inside too that I couldn't yet put into words. I didn't know yet I had known all at the same time. It was a kind of "coming of age" moment for me that I will be deeply indebted to him for. Understanding empathy and compassion and yet not having a clue really how deep that rabbit hole goes has been my life's story.

A deep pull of emotion, even at a young age, was very real to me. I felt it. I knew it. I always have. And truthfully, that is often what makes the work I do so hard. Yet, I see it as a true privilege to hold space for others to feel it too. When we are vulnerable, we allow our true selves to be known. Much like what happens to us when we step out into the light after being in the dark for so long. It's not subtle. It doesn't apologize or burn less bright because we would rather ease in. No, it is like a spotlight, highlighting all the things you don't like about yourself, all the things you feel are negative and ugly and broken. And yet, being known is truly the answer to so many things in life that hold us back and that don't let us thrive. Vulnerability isn't easy when it's you standing in the light.

Think about times in your life when you have been vulnerable. What has that looked like for you? What did it feel like when you allowed yourself to show up that way and be accepted? What did it feel like to show up that way and feel excluded or pushed aside? Do you feel you are in a safe space enough to be vulnerable at home? In your workplace? What are most companies looking for? As a leader, what do you look for in your people? What do companies look for in your leaders? Answering those questions leads us to understanding vulnerability in a different light and to, hopefully, arriving at some solutions as to what it *needs* to look like in the workplace. When we get this right, it opens the door for an opportunity to create a culture that leans into the humanness of its people instead of the perfectionistic tendencies of its expectations. The thing that most results and numbers-driven organizations feel the need to push forward is the very thing that can cause it to break. Back to the question about what most companies look for in their leaders. For most it's transparency, innovation, connection,

Meet Them Where They Are

and this idea of leveraging emotional intelligence. These factors form the backbone of some of the work that we've been doing lately. It has been really eye-opening.

## WHAT OUR RESEARCH HAS SHOWN:

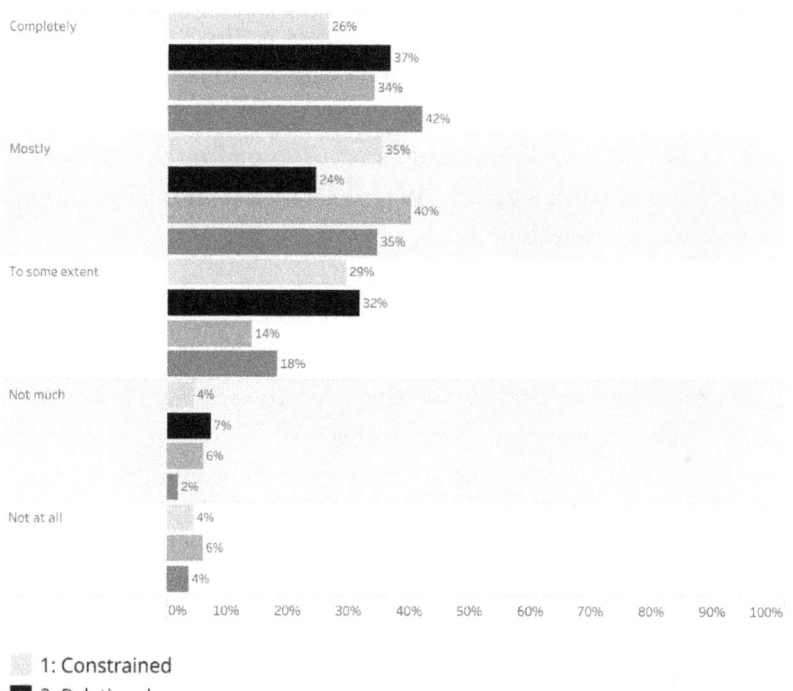

**Figure 12.1: What Vulnerability Looks Like by Leadership Segment**

| Category | 1: Constrained | 2: Relational | 3: Emotionally-Oriented | 4: Outcome-Oriented |
|---|---|---|---|---|
| Completely | 26% | 37% | 34% | 42% |
| Mostly | 35% | 24% | 40% | 35% |
| To some extent | 29% | 32% | 14% | 18% |
| Not much | 4% | 7% | 6% | 2% |
| Not at all | 4% | 6% | 4% | |

1: Constrained
2: Relational
3: Emotionally-Oriented
4: Outcome-Oriented

Note: Q43 Vulnerability in the workplace means team members have the ability to share their emotions, feelings, and perceptions with others and trust that they will be received positively without judgment. Organizations that cultivate vulnerability allow their team members to be human. Do you feel your organization cultivates vulnerability?Audience Audit, & Human Leadership Institute. (2024, September).

How B.R.A.V.E. Human Leadership Behaviors Define Relational Leaders: Leading With Mind and Heart. https://www.thehli.com/research/

**WHAT OUR RESEARCH HAS SHOWN: Only one in three leaders say their organizations completely cultivate vulnerability, a substantial gap from the other letters in our B.R.A.V.E. framework. All four segments and their organizations appear to struggle equally with vulnerability. For more than half of leaders, vulnerability looks like sharing ideas and admitting mistakes at their organizations. Relational Leaders note more expressions of vulnerability at their organizations, especially compared to Constrained Leaders. For example, 68% of Relational Leaders say people admit their mistakes at their organization, but only 39% of Constrained Leaders notice this behavior at their organizations.[1]**

The need for this conversation runs really deep. It's what B.R.A.V.E. Leaders need to focus on today as the idea of vulnerability opens the doors to transparency, innovation, trust, and connection. As we know, nothing really happens without them. So many of us have been taught over time to believe that vulnerability is a bad thing and that it means we are weak. The truth is vulnerability is actually a strength. Only in our ability to be open and real can we show how strong we are in doing so.

In today's fast-paced digital landscape, where connections are often fleeting and superficial, the act of showing vulnerability emerges as a potent tool for leaders. The notion that vulnerability represents weakness is outdated and detrimental to fostering robust workplace relationships. Instead, recognizing vulnerability as a strength can transform leadership dynamics, enhancing trust and authenticity within teams.

*Vulnerability is not about winning or losing; it's about courage and authenticity.*

Mutual exchange, trust, and vulnerability fosters an environment where creativity, innovation, and loyalty flourish. Leaders who embrace their vulnerabilities can dismantle the traditional hierarchies that often stifle open communication and collaboration. The digital age in which we find ourselves today, while offering numerous ways to connect, often lacks the depth found in face-to-face interactions. Leaders face the challenge of building genuine connections through screens and keyboards. By being vulnerable, leaders can bridge this gap, transforming digital communications into channels of meaningful interactions.

Learning to reconceptualize vulnerability requires understanding its impact on trust-building. Trust is foundational in any relationship, but it is especially critical in virtual or hybrid teams where body language and physical cues are absent. When leaders openly share not just successes, but also fears and failures, they demonstrate trustworthiness and reliability—key traits that invite reciprocal openness from team members.

Practically speaking, leaders can showcase vulnerability in digital settings by regularly sharing personal reflections through blogs or videos, actively seeking feedback, and openly discussing their learning journeys. These actions not only humanize the leader but also promote a culture of ongoing learning and adaptability among team members. This culture is how we show up leaning on B.R.A.V.E. behaviors.

Embracing vulnerability helps in navigating the complexities of human emotions in professional settings. Understanding and managing these emotions can significantly enhance decision-making processes and overall team morale. Leaders proficient in emotional intelligence can better support their teams through challenges, leading to improved performance and job satisfaction. We have seen this to be true with so many of our clients. Those who allow themselves to be seen in their humanness are the same ones that find success with their teams that will be long-lasting and truly solid.

In fact, promoting an inclusive culture where every team member feels valued and understood can only be achieved when leaders themselves are open to showing their vulnerabilities. This inclusivity leads to enhanced feelings of belonging among team members, which is vital for sustaining engagement and motivation over time. By integrating these practices into your leadership style, you foster not only a more productive, but also a more harmonious work environment. That environment can be tailored not just for today in the challenges we find around the globe, but for the digital age—a space where authenticity leads and deep connections thrive. The culture to show up and trust others with your vulnerability is the cornerstone to being a successful Relational Leader.

**WHAT OUR RESEARCH HAS SHOWN:**

**Less than half (47%) of leaders say they've seen positive impacts of leadership at their organizations. Two in three believe their leadership presence has contributed to at least one positive outcome. The Relational and Outcome-Oriented Leaders are significantly more likely than Constrained Leaders to see evidence of their leadership contributions.**[2]

A few years ago, I spoke for the largest tire manufacturer in a remote area in New York state. The owner hired me to be the keynote for his annual sales meeting. Twenty-eight distribution location managers would attend and he wanted me to speak for about ninety minutes. He asked that I enter the back of the room that morning and he would call me up when he was finished with his opening message.

As I entered, I saw the backs of twenty-eight heads—all middle aged and older men. I remember immediately being struck with the question: WHY ME? I am sure there are a ton of really great sales-focused male speakers in New York and, yet, he hired me. I was much younger at the time, bisexual, and a woman. I was SURE I had nothing in common with them—any of them. Prejudgment number one. I had a choice in that moment to say, "who cares, I already got paid, just run through this and leave" or "I have a real opportunity to create some connection and change a life today." I chose the second option.

At the end, I closed with an exercise I often use to boost confidence and send people out feeling good about where they landed and what was next for them. It's a sort of confidence resume. Simply put, it's a blank piece of paper numbered 1-10. I asked them to write down their strengths (i.e., what they are good at in their lives.) I gave them about a minute of quiet time to do so. I would then walk around and ask each person to share one with the group. It was always a fun way to end the day. We built up this energy as they would say theirs out loud and I would echo it and then move to the next person. They were getting into it.

When I got about halfway around the group, I got to who was clearly the youngest in the room. His page was totally blank and his head was down staring at the blank paper, pen still lifeless in his hand. I thought to myself, "*Oh, ok ... I get it ... You're too cool for school and didn't want to write anything down. Ok, I see you, tough guy.*" Prejudgment number two. As I approached the front of his table, I asked him to participate anyway. "Ok, go ahead give us one ..." I stopped as he slowly looked up from his paper, and we finally, after a long pause, made eye contact. I saw a tear start down his cheek; his eyes were filling pretty quickly.

He quietly choked out, "I'm stuck. I can't think of any." I paused right then and immediately asked the others in the room to help him fill it out. They did and he wrote down what they yelled out, one after the other. It was emotional for everyone ... **and it was vulnerable**. At that moment, every single person in that room was in touch with their humanity, because Joe (not his real name) felt safe enough in that room that day to be vulnerable, he immediately gave the others the permission to do the same.

When I got home that night, I read through the feedback forms I handed out at the end. I found Joe's. He simply wrote, "Thank you, thank you, thank you. You helped me find strengths I forgot I had. I am going through a very difficult divorce and my wife thinks I am nothing and certainly reminds me often what a failure I am." The importance of the investment in psychological safety and allowing others to utilize the power of relationship needs to be recognized. We know that we can't have one without the other. The bottom line is: vulnerability exists in the hands of trust. Yet, we also know that trust can't exist in a vacuum. Without psychological safety, we have no trust and without trust, we have no vulnerability. Where do we find ourselves showing up in THIS way? Where are we perhaps missing the mark? Think about the people you lead right now in your organization. Is your team equipped to handle the current state of business today? I don't mean technologically or financially. I simply mean emotionally and mentally. Is your team, your family, your peers, and your friends equipped to handle it today? Are they sinking or are they thriving? Are you in a space right now where people are doing really well internally or not? Maybe we need to consider whether or not you even really KNOW how your people are doing in the first place? Have you asked:

***Could embracing your own vulnerabilities be the key to unlocking unprecedented levels of trust within your team?***

We struggle so much with the idea of vulnerability. For most, it's either good or bad. Just like failure, we, as human beings, define that. We attach emotion to outcome and decide whether it's good or bad depending on circumstance and build that construct ourselves. I can tell you, just like failure, vulnerability is neither good nor bad. Vulnerability is a thing in and of itself. Here is a great way to test this for yourself.

Think about people you have known that were your leaders. Think about how you have led throughout your lifetime, think about how people show up, or don't show up in this space of vulnerability when they have the willingness to be real and connect with others. Think about what that looks like. I'm sure we all know somebody who fits that mold. This is where emotional intelligence (EI) assessments, 360 reviews, and the B.R.A.V.E. Human Leadership Indexes are extremely beneficial to identify blind spots that emerge around the lens of vulnerability. I think they happen more often than not. It's our job as leaders to really try to get to the bottom of what's stopping us from being in a place of trust and open, honest connection. Our intention is to help people see, from all sides of the elephant, what this looks like for THEM.

I have noticed that we practice vulnerability much in the way we view vulnerability: that it happens *to* us. We aren't in control, and we are told either it's bad or it's good; there is no in between. We look for it from others and yet aren't fast to let others in to see the parts of us we hide from the outside world. We simply want it from other people, but we're afraid to show it ourselves. We need to really dig into that and understand why. Why am I afraid to do that? Where am I showing up with vulnerability right now and where am I lacking it?

Like failure, or the idea of it anyway, we get to decide how we feel about it and if we see it as good or bad. In order to break free from those ideas and the fear that often dictates how we respond, we need to take some time to reflect and then if we need to, rewrite that story. It also gives us the opportunity to admit and take ownership of our mistakes. When we are vulnerable and truthful about what we didn't do right or times when we fell short of what we had hoped, we show our humanness and stand in a humility that is powerful and telling.

This very act can build relationships stronger than ever. Let's get a couple things clear:

> *Being vulnerable isn't weakness.*
> *Leading from the heart isn't soft or "too touchy-feely."*

Knowing what drives your team members or sharing with them what drives you on a personal level isn't crossing a line. This is antiquated thinking. When we build on the idea of authenticity and vulnerability to share our own story, it is much easier to ask others to share theirs. Make sure there is a safe space for conversation and learn how to be an active listener to give others the permission to be vulnerable. Although they don't *really* need our permission; most people just feel better when they feel like they have it. When you see someone do something scary before you have done it, it's a lot easier to actually try the thing yourself. We call that the "You-Go-First" principle. When someone takes the leap first, others will follow. Like so many people we can go back to examples in history. Roger Bannister stands out as a perfect example of this.

On May 6, 1954, Bannister did what other people had only ever imagined in real life and quite frankly, believed to be impossible. He ran a sub-four-minute mile. At that time, it was considered "Sport's Greatest Goal," by the Daily Telegraph.[3] No one ever thought it was possible before he did it. In fact, they believed it was physically impossible to do so. It took our whole human history for someone to do it the first time. It only took 46 days for someone to do it again.[4] And after that, droves of runners followed suit. Today, it's almost commonplace for elite runners to pace a mile in just under four minutes.

Kathrine Switzer became the first woman to officially run the Boston Marathon in 1967. The year before her, Bobbi Gibb actually ran it too, but had to disguise herself and run without a race entry and bib due to the fact that she wasn't allowed to register as a woman. Switzer became the first woman to wear a bib across the start line. It wasn't because they all of a sudden started allowing women to run. She registered as "K.V. Switzer" because that was actually the way she always signed her name. Being that the name Katherine didn't appear anywhere, there was no way for the race committee to know she was a woman.[5]

During her run, the race manager, Jock Semple, tried to stop Switzer and actually assaulted her for being in the race. He even tried to grab her race bib number to make it so that she would be disqualified and not be able to officially finish. Her trainer and her boyfriend who were both running with her proceeded to shield her to help her cross the finish line. Before that day, it was believed that women couldn't actually run that far. The myths went as far as believing that women couldn't compete in running events longer than 1.5 miles because they were simply physically incapable of doing so because their uterus would fall out. It would, in fact, take five more years before women were actually allowed to officially enter the Boston Marathon.[6]

When we become clear and acknowledge that we can do something, we awaken that piece of us that leans on assuredness and something amazing happens. It's really just science. It's called Reticular Activating System (RAS). This system essentially connects the conscious part of our brain to the subconscious part of our brain and helps us to decide where to put our focus and energy and where to let go of it. It very much follows the premise that you get what you focus on. When you are in the driver's seat of knowing (i.e., in this case knowing you will achieve something you set out to do) you have control over what your RAS keeps and what it gets rid of. Because of this, you are focused only on the things that will help you achieve what you are wanting to do.[7]

When we take the chance to go first, we open the door for others to follow. B.R.A.V.E. Leaders focus time here and work hard on developing this vulnerability muscle. In order to grow this, we have to find openings in our everyday conversations to insert vulnerability and to not be afraid to be our real, authentic selves everywhere we show up. Even if that means trying and failing. When was the last time you did something for the first time? The vulnerability it takes to try something new is enormous. I remember countless times in which I held myself back because I wasn't sure I could do something well enough to try. Perfectionism will always be an "and/both" for me. It was something that made me really great at certain things and yet made me miss out on the new things that I was afraid to try. What if I failed? What if I wasn't good enough? The mental games we play with ourselves can be brutal. Yet, when we harness that power instead of trying to knock it down, the results can be amazing.

The safety mechanisms that organizations with high levels of trust bring result in their ability to report better job performance, increased employee engagement, and higher retention rates. The result here is straightforward: trust leads to open communication, which fosters collaboration and innovation. The safety to be vulnerable directly affects whether innovation will thrive or die on the vine. We don't have to be totally sure. We just need to feel safe enough to try. Trying and failing and getting back up again to try once more even when you are not sure you can succeed, well, that's what champions do. More and more as I get older, I choose to want to win like that.

## CHAPTER 13

# Empathy

The last word that makes up the B.R.A.V.E. Human Leadership Model is EMPATHY. I see compassion as simply "empathy in action." It asks the question: "What is it like to really understand and have the ability to feel and hold space for the suffering and pain of others? To actively listen to their experiences without judgment is to help someone who is sharing their story with you to feel seen and heard. As I said before, while I believe we won't ever be able to perfectly know the intricacies of the path another person has walked before this moment; we can listen and feel enough to understand their pain AND witness their joy. We talk about empathy from the standpoint of not rushing to fix something. Instead, empathy is the ability to really sit with it. To be vulnerable in that moment, to sit with someone in the midst of whatever they're going through and just listen. My Dad was a master at this. I continue to be a work in progress. I bet we would agree that most of us don't do that as well as we probably could.

## WHAT OUR RESEARCH HAS SHOWN:

**Our research shows about half of leaders demonstrate empathy automatically in all of their interactions. Emotionally Focused Leaders (70%) are significantly more likely than Constrained Leaders (40%) to be empathetic as a default.**[1]

In an article from *Entrepreneur* magazine from August 2020 entitled "The Future of Leadership is Empathy-And Companies are Better for it", empathy is described as a behavior and skill that we need to embrace and understand. The first line of the article says "by stepping outside themselves, empathetic leaders are often great communicators and relationship builders".[2] The power behind that is how we can show up this way. How can we bring empathy to the workplace? One of the ways I believe is having a coaching mindset. It's not in managing and pushing people in certain directions. It's learning what it means to coach them to find those directions themselves.

## WHAT OUR RESEARCH HAS SHOWN:

**Nearly all (90%) leaders believe coaching skills are essential or extremely important for strong leadership. Outcome-Oriented and Relational Leaders appear more likely than Constrained Leaders to consider coaching skills indispensable.**[3]

Coaching has been my background for a very long time and I find pure joy in watching someone climb a mountain they thought previously it was too steep. I love watching change happen and to get to possibly be a partial catalyst for that change makes it that much more meaningful. When we really learn how to coach, we can learn to embrace what our clients' actual strengths are first. THEN we can go into the other pieces of figuring out the next steps. Notice that when it comes time for reviews and you talk to people about their performance, we so often do this backwards. We start talking about and focusing on the things they can improve on, glossing over quickly saying things like, "You're really good at THIS, but this is where we need to spend our time." I say it's the other way around. If we embrace and highlight strengths, then we help people really understand what they do well, what they come to the table with, and that we can coach by helping THEM find the answers, not finding answers for them.

Imagine if we build up employees and team members to be stronger in this concept and to be able to go out there and show up this way. This idea of empathy is also in giving them permission to sit in that space and be okay with whatever they need to be. Then, when the time is right, figure out how to fix it together.

## WHAT OUR RESEARCH HAS SHOWN:

**Just under half of leaders say their organizations completely cultivate empathy, and there are no segment differences to note here. About half of leaders notice empathy as offering help when someone is in need, asking questions to better understand others, and seeking to understand rather than make assumptions. Relational Leaders see more examples of empathy in action at their organizations than some of the other segments. They're significantly more likely than Constrained Leaders to offer help when somebody needs it.[4]**

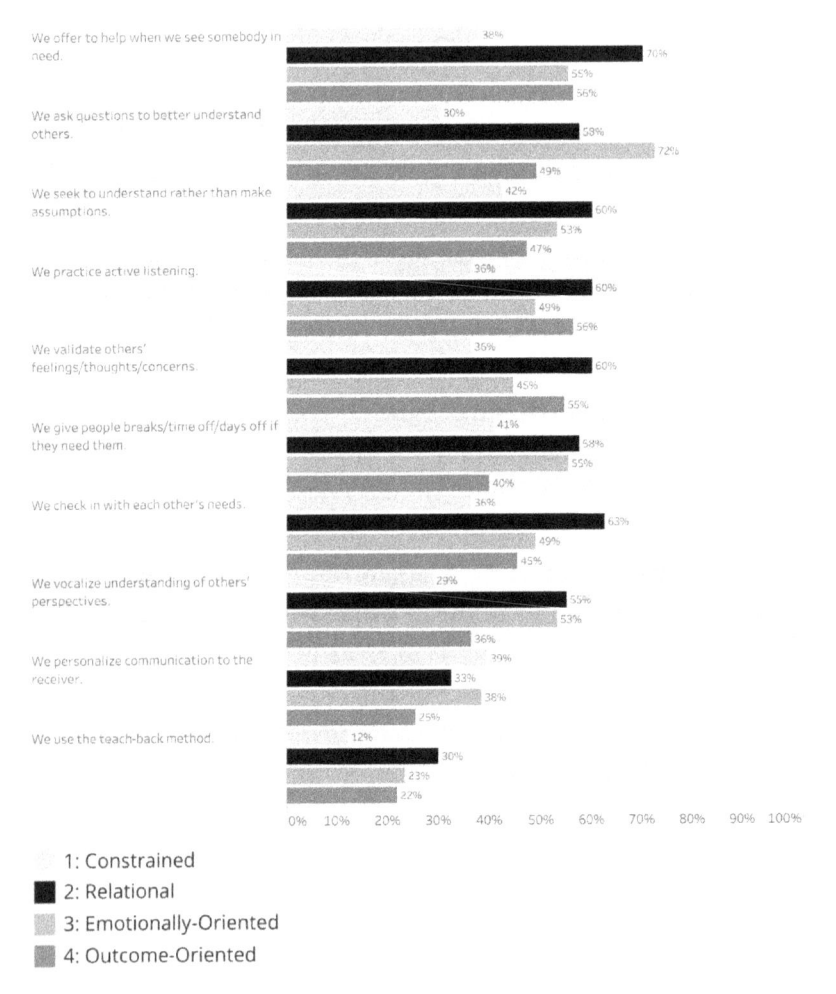

### Figure 13.1: What Empathy Looks Like in Action by Leadership Segment

| Behavior | 1: Constrained | 2: Relational | 3: Emotionally-Oriented | 4: Outcome-Oriented |
|---|---|---|---|---|
| We offer to help when we see somebody in need. | 38% | 70% | 55% | 56% |
| We ask questions to better understand others. | 30% | 58% | 72% | 49% |
| We seek to understand rather than make assumptions. | 42% | 60% | 53% | 47% |
| We practice active listening. | 36% | 60% | 49% | 56% |
| We validate others' feelings/thoughts/concerns. | 36% | 60% | 45% | 55% |
| We give people breaks/time off/days off if they need them. | 41% | 58% | 55% | 40% |
| We check in with each other's needs. | 36% | 63% | 49% | 45% |
| We vocalize understanding of others' perspectives. | 29% | 55% | 53% | 36% |
| We personalize communication to the receiver. | 39% | 33% | 38% | 25% |
| We use the teach-back method. | 12% | 30% | 23% | 22% |

1: Constrained
2: Relational
3: Emotionally-Oriented
4: Outcome-Oriented

Note: Q49 What does empathy look like in your organization? Choose all that apply. Audience Audit, & Human Leadership Institute. (2024, September). How B.R.A.V.E. Human Leadership Behaviors Define Relational Leaders: Leading With Mind and Heart. https://www.thehli.com/research/

**Emotionally Oriented Leaders are significantly more likely to ask questions to better understand others.**

Empathy breeds inclusivity and innovation, while at the same time lessening reactivity, stress, depression, and anxiety. The sticking point is that it needs to come with action. Data continues to show us that we are facing a mental health crisis like we haven't experienced before.[5] We are seeing it from Zoom meetings to boardrooms across the globe. I'm sure you, too, notice a pattern. These same topics keep coming up. More and more, people feel burned out, fatigued, and disengaged. I don't think the issue lies in their inability to get things done or perform. I believe strongly that it lies within how they "human" with each other. We don't need engagement surveys to show us this. We need real life human beings to tell us what they need in order for them to show up fully with an open heart and mind.

There is a greater amount of stress in the workplace, especially after the wave of "return to work" conversations many organizations have been having with their workforce. For the first time in almost four years, many employers are pushing for their teams to come back into the office full time.[6] According to an article published by the Anxiety and Depression Association of America (ADAA) : "Limeade Institute surprisingly found that 100% of respondents indicated some degree of anxiety about returning to the workplace. The survey included 4,553 full-time employees from Australia, France, Germany, the United Kingdom, and the United States who were working on-site before the pandemic but now were working from home. The top return-to-work sources of anxiety included: exposure to COVID-19 (77%), less flexibility (71%), and commuting to work (68%). These results indicate that most of us are not only worried about our health and safety, but also concerned about losing our newfound autonomy and flexibility."[7] As we watched this stress increase through the global pandemic, Mental Health America found that in 2022, 81% of workers report that workplace stress affects their mental health, compared to 78% of respondents in 2021.[8]

As a leader, it is critical to wrap your head around how you can positively affect the people around you, knowing that mental health is an important issue to understand. Empathy in leadership is about having grace and understanding around these topics and giving your people the gift of compassion. Learn and participate in giving it by understanding its importance to getting the best from your team. Meet others where they are and, in any way possible, lean into grace and compassion, remembering we never know others' circumstances.

---

### CASE STUDY

Susan Savini, Director of Critical Care Nurse Practitioners, Intensive Care Unit (ICU), Chester County Hospital, Penn Medicine

---

*Jen: Tell us a little bit about your background and how you got to where you are today.*

**Susan**: I became a nurse 37 years ago. I have always been fascinated with anatomy and physiology and I loved being in school. After I obtained my Registered Nursing (RN) degree, I immediately pursued a Bachelor of Science in Nursing (BSN). Several years later I enrolled in a Family Nurse Practitioner (NP) program and graduated with a Master's degree in Nursing. In the years that followed, my attraction to education led me to a post Master's program with a second NP degree in acute care and a Doctorate in nursing practice. I continue to enjoy various roles as adjunct faculty at several local universities teaching nursing at all levels.

I have always loved being a nurse. It would be remiss of me if I did not insert here that my most important and cherished job, though, has been being a Mom. Humbly, I hope people would describe me as being good at both of these jobs, mom first, then nurse. I have thoroughly loved every moment of being both.

I am the Director of Critical Care Nurse Practitioners in the Intensive Care Unit (ICU). I am a Doctorate Prepared Nurse Practitioner certified in both family practice and acute care. I oversee a group of 15 highly skilled NPs who cover an adult ICU 24/7 (meaning we have a fully staffed day shift and night shift).

Some of my duties as Director involve scheduling, HR & certification compliance, attendance at relevant task force meetings, payroll, staff evaluations and coordination of bimonthly staff meetings. My administrative duties comprise approximately 20% of my time at work. Mostly, though, I am clinical, which means I am usually in the ICU caring for patients and I am included in the daily schedule of ICU work responsibilities.

Our role involves total care of critically ill adults in the ICU in collaboration with our ICU Intensivist Physicians. We enjoy a very collegial relationship with our attending physicians who allow us to largely function independently and to the full scope of our practice.

Additionally, we are responsible for running the Rapid Response and Code Blue teams. These calls are designated to have medical help available within 5 minutes anywhere in the hospital during any emergency or cardiac arrest event. In essence, we are the hospital's internal 911 system. When the beeper calls, we must stop what we are doing and immediately respond to where we are summoned. Anticipating the emergency, we are responding to can sometimes be a harrowing experience.

Surprisingly, in this position, I have seen very little turnover rate. Only two people have left during my tenure here, both due to relocation secondary to spousal employment.

I have been in this position for seventeen years. Prior to this position, I worked in a cardiothoracic ICU taking care of heart surgery patients. The entirety of my nursing career has been in critical care.

***Jen***: *Obviously you have had to have a lot of practice with empathy. Tell us what that looks like for you:*

**Susan**: Empathy is a concept that I feel is often interchanged with sympathy. I believe empathy is so much deeper and much more robust than sympathy. Sympathy means you are feeling "for" a person. Empathy assumes you are actually feeling what another person feels. Empathy, then, is feeling "with" them. Empathy is being present, in the moment. It is an intimate sharing experience based on feelings so much deeper than "Oh, that's sad" or "I'm sorry you're going through this".

In my job, the precursor to empathy has to be non-judgementalism. This can be a difficult concept. We all bring our past experiences and lessons to our daily life, right? If we feel a certain way, negative or positive, it can affect our ability to be empathetic. For example, if you think people with addictions are weak or lazy, maybe you shouldn't be working in a drug treatment center, knowing you struggle with empathy in that particular patient population.

Empathy in my job means trying to put myself in a patient's position. Asking myself "how would I feel/respond/react if this was happening to me or someone I love?" It means trying to feel exactly what the patient is feeling. At times, it is beneficial to think back on my own experiences and how I felt at that time. For example, when I am in a situation where a parent is dying, I think back to the grief I experienced when my own parents passed. Sometimes, I may even share something personal to let the patients know that I have been through a similar situation. I am essentially, in that moment, feeling "with" them, not only "for" them. I am fully present.

*Jen*: *Do you have any stories of empathy that really stand out to you?*

**Susan**: Throughout my career, both as a nurse and as a provider, I have always been drawn to end of life care. I consider myself a staunch advocate for comfort and reverence at the end of life. As healthcare providers dealing with a patient's death, we are like uninvited guests, fully immersed in the family dynamics of strangers during the most intimate and sacred situations. While this may cause discomfort for some, it has always created a desire within me to be present for both the patient and their families. How honored and privileged I have been to care for not only my patients gently and compassionately at this time, but their significant others as well. End of life care means you are treating the patient AND their family during a tremendously difficult situation. I'd like to think I have managed many end-of-life situations well.

I also try hard to show empathy when I know a patient needs to undergo something that is uncomfortable, scary, or downright painful. Especially if the event is something I am doing TO them. I typically spend time thoroughly explaining and talking to them continually through the procedure.

I often will utilize guided imagery, deep breathing, or distraction techniques in an attempt to alleviate their anxiety. I frequently ask patients what their happy place is and use guided imagery to pretend we are there. I have found myself on a golf course in Ireland, the beach, a library, the race track, and a casino while "pretending" with my patients. Oh, the places I've been!

My favorite imagery technique when I am placing a feeding tube through the nose to the stomach, is to pretend we are at Dairy Queen sipping a milkshake. I have the patient decide on chocolate or vanilla, have them close their eyes and when the feeding tube reaches their throat (which makes some people gag), I tell them to take a big swallow of their shake. I tell them it's cold, thick and delicious, swallow now! I have snaked many a tube into the esophagus (gagging now over) using guided imagery with a milkshake. And I always ask the patient when I'm done if we are still friends. One patient replied yes but his wife would be jealous he took me on a date to Dairy Queen.

In these situations, I try to be empathetic, imagining how I would feel or react to something uncomfortable, scary, or painful. I imagine I'm in their shoes. I hope someone would keep me informed and work hard to distract me when I'm scared. If I were the patient undergoing a procedure, I'd like to know that the provider working on me is present, with me in the moment.

Being empathetic in my job sometimes means letting the patient see my humanness. I don't want a patient encounter to feel like a business transaction. I want to make time if they need someone to sit with them. Even when I feel overwhelmed and busy, I want the patient to know that what they have to say is important and that I want to hear it. Sometimes this means sitting down in a chair even when my duties outside of their room are piling up. It means often repeating the same information several times, knowing they are stressed and not comprehending everything they are being told.

I have often found myself expressing empathy and being present in the moment by participating in prayer, song, and other bedside activities when invited by the patient or their family. I always participate when asked. One particular case I remember was when my patient was dying and the family asked me to join their circle of hand holding and pray. I gladly agreed. I did not know, however, that this prayer would involve loud music, tambourines, and wild arm movements. Imagine the questioning I received as I left the room. My nursing colleagues were watching the whole time!

**Jen**: *Knowing empathy's importance to the work you do; is there a way you can find to balance yourself or make sure you don't fall into empathy fatigue where it all becomes just too much?*

**Susan**: Aside from skill and the generalized fund of knowledge required to care for the critically ill, empathy comes in a close second. By its very nature, critical care nursing/medicine comes with a hefty dose of trauma, loss, and grief. Patients deserve empathy. Their families deserve empathy.

People don't want to be sick; they don't want to be in the hospital. Healthcare workers are not observing people as their best selves. Typically, if you are in the hospital, it is because something is WRONG. Nobody would choose to be in this situation. That alone is deserving of empathy.

I have many times been overcome with the sheer amount of death I have witnessed. I would be lying if I said it did not weigh heavily on me at times. It makes me think of my own mortality and I find myself wondering how my end will be. When my children were younger, I remember driving home from work some nights after a particularly stressful or sad day and thinking, "*Nope, not ready to go home yet, I'm not done crying*". I would drive around for a few more minutes so as not to upset my family.

Being empathetic can be very emotionally draining. Not only are you dealing with your own feelings, but then taking on the feelings of others as well. That being said, I can honestly say when I expend energy being empathetic, I feel it is energy well spent. Most days if I were to ask myself, "Did I help anyone today?", the answer is a resounding

YES. The outcome far outweighs the energy exerted. It's like a tough workout, it's really hard to get through and sometimes it actually hurts but look how good it makes you feel afterwards. Being empathetic at work makes me feel good. Being in healthcare is so rewarding. I honestly cannot imagine doing anything else.

When I am overwhelmed or overstimulated (beeper, call bells, telephones, monitor alarms), I seek out solitude and a quiet place. It has taken me a long time to embrace the concept of self-care and downtime. Knowing I can seek quiet and solitude helps me to be energetic at work. I have come to absolutely love my time off and I don't feel guilty if I just want to be alone for a bit. Setting boundaries outside of work has sometimes been challenging for me, although I think I am starting to realize the benefit of it. It only took me (almost) 40 years to get here!

I give myself permission to detach when I need to. I also have an awareness of the people close to me who are tolerant of listening to my sad stories, and those who would rather not hear about it, realizing some stories are not for the faint of heart. A decent and reliable support system is a must! Having things to do outside of work and my hobbies (playing guitar, exercise, yoga, crochet, jigsaw and crossword puzzles, and being outside in nature) help to clear my mind and reset my compassion fatigue. I decided during COVID that I would teach myself how to play the piano. When I learned guitar, I never learned how to read music. How hard could it be? Suffice it to say, I will not be quitting my day job anytime soon.

***Jen***: *How is your job different now than before COVID? What have you found to have changed over the past few years not just in the workplace, but in the whole world regarding empathy now?*

***Susan***: The healthcare workforce has been traumatized by the COVID pandemic. In many ways, we will never be the same. So many opinions, judgements, changes. Spending two years fighting an invisible enemy took its toll on everyone involved. The fear and the unknown were at times debilitating. Some people left healthcare altogether. If I had a dime every time I heard someone say, "This is not what I signed up for."

I came to abhor that comment. I felt disappointed to watch nurses leave the bedside during the pandemic. I know the fear, grief, fatigue, and exhaustion that COVID brought. It took my brother from me. I spent many days calling family members to tell them their loved one has passed away (back when we were not allowing visitors in the hospital). I watched in horror as a large freezer was delivered out back when we ran out of room in the morgue to place the bodies. I also know that this is exactly what we signed up for, caring for the sick and dying. Having empathy. For all the agony that pandemic placed on me, I would still do it again. It's what I was taught to do.

Further fueling the flame was the COVID division of our nation as a whole. Healthcare front line workers were initially lauded as heroes in the beginning, but eventually some of our patients were skeptical of our intentions. Caring for people who ridiculed our services/protocols/practices made many staff feel deflated and underappreciated. More than once, I heard the phrase "we went from the heroes to the zeros".

Sadly, I can say I felt this way myself towards the end of the pandemic. It was sometimes difficult to express empathy when I was insulted by patients for wearing protective gear and I witnessed an uptick in patient and visitor aggressive behavior requiring interventions/de-escalation by hospital security. I remember feeling uneasy at work and often wondering what the heck was happening to our world.

Difficult situations still require empathy in healthcare. Empathy cannot just be given to those who are being cordial to us. During difficult situations, it sometimes helps to make an effort to not take things personally. It is also helpful to try and think about all the extraneous things that may be making a patient less than pleasant. Again, we are not seeing people as their best selves, maybe they need someone to give them a pass on their behavior.

Overall, I feel that the concept of empathy is struggling in the world in general. It seems so many people are intolerant and angry. Just watching the news is so discouraging. There seems to be a sense of entitlement and selfishness that I don't seem to remember, at least not to this extent. I think back to the months immediately following the 9/11 attacks. Strangers just seemed so soft and caring then, we were all united and felt protective of one another. Where did that go? Now, it seems many people are suspicious and accusatory, which makes ordinary situations feel defensive. I wish we could go back to the feeling that we are all in this together.

Enrollment in medical and nursing education has declined significantly. This saddens me greatly. My career in healthcare has been such an exhilarating and rewarding ride. I love it and I want other people to love it too. I feel protective of my profession, and I want other people to embrace and protect it too.

***Jen***: *What would you tell a younger person today who was just entering healthcare as a profession?*

**Susan**: When I was in high school, I did not have any thoughts or desires to be a nurse. In fact, I was afraid of doctors and hated the smell of hospitals. I landed in nursing school because my parents could not afford to send me to college. I took an anatomy course as an elective my senior year of high school and I could not get my head out of the book. SO, my parents and guidance counselor decided I should be a nurse. I enrolled in nursing school with a big chip on my shoulder because it was not my choice.

I will forever be eternally grateful that my parents saw something in me that I could not see in myself at the time. I was meant to take care of sick people. From the first day of clinicals in nursing school (with my starched uniform dress, white pantyhose and yes, the white nurses cap), I have embraced this wonderful profession and to this day, I still feel proud to say I am a nurse. I am proud I landed in a noble and trustworthy profession.

Had it not been for my parents, I would not have had the opportunity or experience to care for them when they were sick and dying. I would not have been able to tend to my disabled brother as he lay dying of COVID in my ICU. And I certainly would not be sharing these stories of my professional journey with you. I was so lucky to have them all, my family. Because of them, I know love. I know how to show kindness, compassion, and empathy. I thank God every day for the gift they were in my life.

I often present to high school students considering a profession in healthcare. I speak about my professional journey and what it has meant to me. I encourage them to find a profession they love and commit every day to try and be a little better at it than the day before. Choose something that you do not dread going to do, I tell them, and something you'd do even if you aren't getting paid to do it.

That's what I did.

⸻

The conversation with Susan reminded me why this work is so critically important today, possibly more than ever. In some ways, I think we use empathy as an expectation without truly knowing how to best embody it. I witnessed moments in my own life where empathy would have been the best answer and, yet I let my wall stay just strong enough to stop me from doing so in order to keep me safe. I can't even explain how I thought I would feel "safe" or how just not feeling empathy was a better answer because any time I have secured that wall, it only meant that in reality what I have done was to completely shut others out instead. I have felt lonely, isolated, and disconnected when I needed to feel connection the most. Empathy can be scary. It's the vulnerability of letting our innermost, sacred feelings be exposed. Yet, wounds don't heal fully if they never get air. Empathy never can grow and flourish if we only ever keep it to ourselves.

The gift of empathy is that it doesn't just make the person you give it to feel lighter or less on an island, it rubs off and it gives you an opportunity to feel that way too. There is something powerful about the feeling we get when we help to lift others out of the pain and suffering, they may be stuck in. So often, I think we give what we so badly want to receive ourselves. What if just that act of giving it to someone else allows us to actually get it too—like a buy one, get one free jar of empathy: a gift to be shared with each other.

## WHAT OUR RESEARCH HAS SHOWN:

**Two in three leaders say there are things that get in the way of them being empathetic towards others. Top barriers include not wanting to say the wrong thing (20%) and having different lived experiences (17%). Constrained Leaders list more challenges with empathy than the other segments.**[9]

To actually achieve this level of empathy, we need to become better listeners. Not passively, while typing an email, or reading a report, or watching a video. We need to learn to listen more effectively with all of our senses if we are able. My Mom used to tell me to look at her when she was talking. Ten-year-old me had no clue why that was important. A "few" decades later, I get it.

Active listening involves more than hearing words; it involves understanding the complete message being conveyed. In a digital setting where non-verbal cues are limited or absent, honing this skill ensures that leaders do not just passively consume words, but engage with the underlying sentiments and ideas. It's about creating a space where dialogue flows freely and everyone feels understood—an indispensable aspect in managing remote teams and digital interactions.

Developing one's emotional intelligence quotient (known as EQ) is another critical step for empathetic leaders today. EQ enables one to navigate the complexities of human emotions in professional settings, maintaining composure, and making informed decisions amidst emotional undercurrents. It also empowers leaders to handle interpersonal dynamics with tact and sensitivity, which is pivotal in maintaining team morale and fostering an inclusive workplace culture.[10]

**WHAT OUR RESEARCH HAS SHOWN:**

**Over half of leaders (57%) want most to understand what inspires their direct reports and what they need to be productive. They also want to understand professional goals (52%).**

**Relational Leaders want to know the most about the people they lead. Constrained Leaders cite the least.[11]**

Empathy extends beyond understanding from an intellectual standpoint to emotionally connecting with others' experiences. In virtual or written communications, where it's easy to misinterpret tone or intent, empathy allows leaders to bridge the gap between what is said and what is meant. This connection fosters trust and openness within teams, making it easier to tackle challenges collaboratively.

I like to think about empathy as a big game of Manhunt that we used to play as kids in our neighborhood. Manhunt is like hide and seek, but in reverse. Usually, we'd head out when it was getting dark. One or a small group of us would hide and the rest of us would go out and find the others one-by-one. The game ended when either you were found or you made it back to home base safely without being tagged. Sometimes, the rule would be that if you found someone on the hiding team, you could hide with them instead to form an alliance. To me, empathy is like climbing quietly into that hiding spot next to someone and not needing to say a word, but letting them know that you're there and you'll sit there with them for as long as it takes to be found.

If each of us practices that kind of empathy, if we live out the five tenets of B.R.A.V.E Human Leadership, and if we recognize the importance of each of these five words, we would never, ever lose sight of influencing a society that no longer craves connection, but cultivates a sense of belonging everywhere we show up. This is the crossroad at which compassion meets humanity. Where we live and breathe with emotion, even in the workplace, and we're not afraid to be authentic in our leadership and heart-centered in our influence.

B.R.A.V.E. Human Leadership is what we need right now more than ever. Bringing these behaviors to the surface today will, beyond a shadow of a doubt, bring us beyond the brink of real change. We haven't even scratched the surface of all we are capable of. Regardless of how far we have come, or how far we still have yet to go, I'm in it with you. It is my hope that together, being B.R.A.V.E. will be the legacy that we choose to leave for all those who come after us for generations.

# PART III

## CHAPTER 14

# Where We Go From Here

If you're like me, you like to have a plan; perhaps even a plan for when that plan fails or is thrown out the window. Yet, some would say I am fairly adept on my feet, agile, and flexible in a moment's notice. Maybe I am both … more than likely, probably neither. I think it depends on the scenario. One of the most important lessons I have learned throughout my life in business has been that need for "and/both." More than one thing can be true at a time. When that is the case, the importance lies in figuring out where to put your attention in the moment.

Just last year, I was reminded of actually living out the notion of "and/both" when I realized I could hold grief and joy at the same time when my Dad died on a Thursday and my brother got married that Saturday. I have lived out the feeling of "and/both" when I had to make the tough choice to put down my dog, Macy, when she was sick. I KNEW it was best for her because she was suffering, and also knew how much I would miss her. I have stood in the midst of a rain shower while the sunbeams, just like the raindrops, were beating down on the tops of my shoulders. That double rainbow that followed was worth all of it.

"What's next?" is just like this. Like it always has been. Maybe it will be no big surprise or grand finale or major change of scenery. No music or fanfare or hype. Life will continue to be full of twists and turns and knowns and unknowns. It will continue to morph and change just like we have lived through our whole lives so far. What's next is simply what we imagine it will be. No more, no less. The difference between then and now is one very critical thing:

**YOU get to decide, and then YOU must take action for it to matter.**
**There's no getting around that.**
**The decision means nothing if you do nothing with it.**

Literally and figuratively. You get to decide how the next chapter reads. You can decide to read these ideas, put the book down, and go right back to where you have been. You can choose to hide behind the difficulty or grab hold of the moment. You can shrink or reinforce your wall, because oftentimes either one feels safer than doing nothing. You can do all of those things at the same time. What you *can't* do is pretend you don't know.

As we move forward into the future, into the age of artificial intelligence (AI) and digital transformation—that once was only imagined on episodes of the Jetsons—is upon us. All the while, I am still waiting for that shower conveyor belt to speed up the morning routine. What we do with it now is everyone's best guess. Here is what I know for sure: what will prove to be the most important skills we can have in this time and space are people skills.

An article published in *Forbes* on December 17, 2023, stated, "Human skills are more critical in an AI environment as robots and algorithms rely on human inputs and do not have the ability to process emotions".[1] Aneesh Raman, a speechwriter who worked for President Obama, recently spoke at a Talent Connect conference in the United Kingdom saying that we must focus on "building a more human world of work in the age of AI".[2] He went on to say that "in the farming era and industrial revolution era we needed muscles, in the digital era we needed our brain and *in the AI era we need relationships!*"[3] Even the CEO of LinkedIn, Ryan Roslansky, had something to say about human-centered focus in the midst of a tech transformation stating, "Our data shows 92% of US executives believe people skills are more important than ever".[4] So, how do we see human skills showing up now?

While AI excels at processing large amounts of data and performing repetitive tasks, it lacks the innate creativity and imagination of humans. Human creativity is essential for generating novel ideas, solving complex problems, and driving innovation. We also possess the ability to critically analyze information, evaluate arguments, and make reasoned judgments. Critical thinking skills are crucial for interpreting AI-generated insights, identifying biases and limitations in AI systems, and making informed decisions.

Clearly, AI lacks emotional intelligence, empathy, and understanding of human emotions. Human skills like we highlight in our B.R.A.V.E. Human Leadership model like empathy, active listening, and interpersonal communication are essential for building meaningful relationships, resolving conflicts, and providing compassionate care: all things that AI can't do alone. AI systems operate based on algorithms and predictive modeling, without inherent moral judgment (which needs to be actively trained by humans into the underlying models.) Human ethical reasoning and moral values are necessary for guiding the development and deployment of AI technologies in ways that align with societal values and norms.

As much as change is hard, we are in a time where we must be, and are, capable of adapting to changing circumstances, learning new skills, and evolving over time. In the rapidly changing landscape of technology, human adaptability is crucial for staying relevant, responding to unexpected challenges, as well as seizing new opportunities. This is the lifeblood of future innovation.

Because AI lacks cultural awareness and contextual understanding that can lead to potential biases and misunderstandings, human cultural competence and a diversity of perspectives are critical for ensuring that AI technologies are inclusive, equitable, and culturally sensitive.

Where we go from here is unclear in a world in the midst of an AI revolution. It is a balance act, or dance, that we will do together to make sure that human skills complement the capabilities of AI. When we bring our unique human skills such as creativity, critical thinking, emotional intelligence, ethical reasoning, adaptability, and collaboration, we can actually move the needles of workplace culture forward, faster. By harnessing the strengths of both humans and AI, we can create a more inclusive, ethical, and sustainable future. To that end, we are afforded the option of possibility in the midst of the unknown. And what's so amazing about that is how many people we can positively affect along the way.

What can we do now to set ourselves up for success? Building stronger connections and communities involves a multi-faceted approach that encompasses both individual actions and collective efforts. How can you foster more active listening? When people feel heard, they are more likely to engage positively. How can you make sure you are creating safe spaces where people feel safe to express their thoughts, feelings, and concerns openly? We try to do this through different ways to have open forums or discussion groups. We call these "leader roundtables," compassionate listening sessions, or connective coaching conversations.

What we have seen across a broad spectrum of industries, companies, and leadership teams is that they work.

Building strong communities also works best when we promote a diverse, inclusive, and equitable culture. Celebrating differences and creating environments where everyone feels valued and respected should be a part of everyday connection, not a separate initiative. In doing so, the use of collaboration across work groups or departments is a way to make all voices heard. Working together toward a common goal is a powerful way to instill community and connection into your team rather quickly. To highlight your team's diversity, organize events that celebrate different cultures, traditions, and perspectives within the community. This can help break down barriers and foster understanding among teams. This isn't the ONLY thing. It has to be more than that.

Establishing support networks within the community to provide assistance to those in need, whether it's emotional support, practical help, or resources, is an even more powerful way to build stronger connections. By promoting education and awareness on important issues such as mental health, environmental sustainability, and social justice, you allow for learning to take place. Knowledge empowers individuals to take action and make positive changes in their workplace and broader communities. By focusing on these areas and encouraging active participation from team members, we can work towards building stronger connections and communities that are more resilient, inclusive, and supportive both inside the workplace and beyond.

*Change is not always bad. Trust that the process is on purpose. Perhaps that conveyor belt shower is just around the corner. And if it is, I will be right here ... patiently waiting.*

## CHAPTER 15

# How B.R.A.V.E. Behaviors Dictate Performance

Beyond the recognition that AI will transform our lives across all landscapes, we can't leave out the mental capacity we rely on in and of ourselves. The overarching theme of this book is the integration of B.R.A.V.E. behaviors into your leadership style over the next six months to a year without sacrificing performance outcomes. By consistently applying these principles, you will not only improve team dynamics but also elevate your organizational culture to new heights. This is the goal we have built this framework around:

*To help those at any level of leadership,
sport or life to pursue a higher level of performance
BECAUSE of increasing B.R.A.V.E. behaviors, not in spite of them.*

Throughout my early career as a sports psychology consultant for professional athletes, seven-year-olds, and everyone in between, I was fascinated by the way the brain functioned and the wiring between our brains and our bodies. The mental/physical link in which we perform will always be one of power to me. Part of what I believe the Performance Enhancing Drugs (PED) era has been about is the fact that we can only take our physical bodies so far. We can only become as fast, as strong, and as agile as our physical selves allow. There will always be a cap on physical performance that leads to the push for competitors to find a way around it. There will NEVER likely be a cap on the potential of the brain. Finding ways to harness that potential is how we get the best from ourselves and our teams.

I have always found a direct parallels between the workplace and the playing field. I believe there is a vast similarity between the team dynamics, culture, leadership, and performance of a work team and an athletic team and between an executive of a company and a high-level sports coach . These are the threads that we focus on daily. As our proprietary research has shown us, you can score high on your ability to focus on performance outcomes and not on the people, or vice versa. The most successful leaders and cultures, however, find a way to do both.

This got me thinking. I have worked with many professional and Olympic level athletes in my career. They know the importance and impact of leadership and culture firsthand. They understand what performance at a championship level means. A few of them have graciously allowed me the time to take this research a step further and find out how they see this play out on their field. What follows in this chapter are five case study interviews with former Olympic and Professional athletes from four different sports and how B.R.A.V.E. Human Leadership principles played a roll in their success.

> **CASE STUDY**
>
> Carli Lloyd, two-time Olympic gold medalist, two-time FIFA Women's World Cup champion, two-time FIFA Player of the Year, four-time Olympian and newly elected to the US National Soccer Hall of Fame.

I had the pleasure of spending some time with Carli Lloyd as she was retiring from her pro soccer career. Here is our conversation about how performance meets B.R.A.V.E. Human Leadership behaviors.

*Jen*: Carli, as always, it's great to connect. You have had an incredible career as a very accomplished athlete. Tell us about what made you fall in love with soccer.

*Carli*: My parents signed me up to play soccer at the age of five. They also signed me up to play other sports and activities: swimming, piano, dance, softball, and I was incredibly active playing any and all sports in my neighborhood. But soccer was my first love, and it was all I cared about. My parents didn't play or come from a soccer background, but the sport challenged me every time I stepped on the field. It required different skill sets and thinking and the best thing of all is I was a competitor and always wanted to push myself to be better. Soccer helped me feel confident, strong and tough whenever I was playing.

*Jen*: Along the lines of less tangible skills, what aspects of the human connection do you think made you thrive as an Olympic/pro athlete?

*Carli*: Teams are incredible to be part of because everyone is different, and the best teams bring out everyone's individual brilliance and merge it into one group that is on a mission to achieve one goal-- winning. Every great team that I have been part of was committed to the collective goal and each and every player accepted their role to the best of their ability. The US Women's National Team was created on a winning mentality and that is what brought us all together throughout the years and how we pushed each to be better every single day.

*Jen*: Because of that high team standard, how do you feel leadership affected your performance, both yours and those around you, your coaches, etc.?

*Carli*: I truly believe in order to lead others you need to be able to lead yourself first. That means being comfortable in your own skin, being disciplined and consistent in everything that you do, having a growth mindset and being accountable. Once you turn habits into your everyday routine, you can then lead by example. I was not a very vocal leader, but I lead by example striving to do the right things on and off the field. I would never ask my teammates to do something that I wasn't already doing.

*Jen*: How do factors like the behaviors around Belonging, Resilience, Authenticity, Vulnerability and Empathy (B.R.A.V.E.) directly impact you as a player?

*Carli*: Belonging on a team is creating the right culture within to accept everyone as they are. What makes teams so special is that everyone is different, and it is important to have some connections with teammates big or small. The reality is, not everyone is going to be friends or choose to hang out with one other and that is ok. Once I stepped over the line to play, I was going to go to battle for all of my teammates.

I would have never made the national team if I didn't learn how to be resilient. This has been the number one trait in my career that kept me going for 17 years. I learned quickly that nothing was a guarantee and that you have to fight and prove yourself day in and day out. The difficult situations that I faced would feel like it was an impossible mountain to climb at first and then once you get past one obstacle you get stronger and stronger with each one that comes your way. I started to invite challenging situations because I knew I would come out on the other side better for it.

In a world where you can be pulled in many different directions and change who you are depending on the situation you are in, I believe that being authentic and living by the values you believe in is the best approach, which allows you to be at your best. Being true to oneself has more of a lasting impression than someone who values following others and their opinions.

I found that being vulnerable was difficult for me on the US Women's National team. I never wanted to show any sign of weakness by talking about my emotions and I shared those emotions with my support system away from the team. The US women's national team was an incredibly hard environment to be in that either made you or broke you. Majority of the time I was numb and emotionless, like a machine. Toward the end of my career, I started to break down some of the walls and open up to my teammates and it felt good. I think there is balance needed from a personal and team standpoint to be vulnerable that allows everyone around you to trust you and help the team connect.

When I think about empathy in my career, I immediately think about our opening game vs Thailand in the 2019 World Cup. We beat them 13-0 and we got a lot of criticism for running the score up and celebrating goals. As I watched most of the game from the bench and eventually came on and scored a goal as well, I couldn't help but think about how bad I felt for the goalkeeper and the players. I was highly competitive but there is a human element that hits you. When the final whistle blew, I immediately went up to the goalkeeper and gave her a hug and told her to stay strong and keep going because I couldn't imagine how she was feeling. We hugged and the photos from that moment are what sport is all about. Competing but also supporting one another. Five years later I saw some of those same players and the goalkeeper at the FIFA congress in Thailand and they were all so happy to see me and my pregnant belly! Sports unite people and it is so important to be humble in successful moments and in moments when you fail.

*Jen*: How did all of that inform your career after you started down the path of retirement? What are you doing now that directly is BECAUSE of what you experienced as a pro/Olympic athlete?

*Carli*: The moment I picked up a soccer ball at the age of five, I could have never dreamed of where this sport has taken me and all of the life lessons it has taught me. I owe everything to this sport. I got to travel the world, meet incredible people, experience success and failure, learn to believe in myself, learn to stay true to who I am, learn that nothing will ever be handed to me and to persevere through challenging situations. Not many athletes get to go out on their own terms, and I was grateful I was able to do that. I was ready to turn the page and be able to live my life. Soccer was never tied to who I was as a person, it was what I did for a living. I am very blessed to be able to stay busy doing speaking engagements, my own CL10 Soccer Clinics, TV studio analyst work, and opportunities with my sponsors. Everything that I went through and learned throughout my life of playing soccer for 34 years prepared me for my life after soccer.

---

Carli is a role model for so many, young and old, and is a brilliant example for what B.R.A.V.E. really is all about. Everything she continues to do because of it is pure gold. She is a great human on and off the field and I have no doubt that everything that comes next for Carli will be a win.

---

> **CASE STUDY**
>
> Joey Lye, Olympic Bronze Medalist with Team Canada (Softball), TEDx Speaker, Coach

Joey is a Leadership Coach, Olympic Bronze Medalist, and TEDx speaker who specializes in high performance consulting, speaking engagements, and workshops. Here is her perspective on how performance and people excel

*Jen*: Joey, it's great to chat with you again. Tell us about what made you fall in love with your sport and with being an athlete.

*Joey*: I was introduced to movement and body control through things like gymnastics, swimming, and skating at a very young age and transitioned to team sports around the age of seven or eight; that is when my love of sport truly began. I played on every team possible in elementary school and middle school. In high school, I finally settled on four: ice hockey, field hockey, soccer, and softball, while also competing on travel hockey and softball teams. I fell in love with the idea of working toward ridiculously high expectations with a group of people. I fell in love with the endless pursuit of evolution and excellence. No matter how much I learned about each sport, there was always more to take in. I was told I had to pick a sport to focus on for the college recruiting process. I was playing hockey and softball the most seriously, but I could not choose just one.

I found a school that would let me play both and know that my love for teamwork and the pursuit of excellence are what motivated me to complete my homework assignments. I love playing hockey more than anything else and still play to this day. There's nothing like it. Nothing else matters when you're out there. Softball was a close second. I ended up competing in softball for 27 years, spending my final 12 years with Team Canada and retiring on the podium at the Olympic Games, in Tokyo, with Canada's first ever Olympic medal in softball hanging around my neck. I love how sport challenges you and that it changes you. I love that in order to evolve, you must get outside of your comfort zone. Most of all, I love the relationships I've built through sport - both with others and with myself.

*Jen*: You talk about how important those relationships are in your keynotes and trainings, so let's dive deeper on that. What aspects of the human connection made you thrive as an Olympic/pro athlete?

*Joey*: I felt and appreciated the human connection piece of sport throughout my whole career and learned that, if I wanted to be my very best, it was not a solitary journey. As the Olympics became a real possibility, our team continued to evolve its culture, and we all worked to become the best versions of ourselves. My teammates were such a big part of my journey and, without a doubt, enhanced my ability to perform. From eye contact that held immense depth on the field to learning and being what one another needed in challenging moments, those who watched us perform in Tokyo could feel the love we had for one another from halfway around the world through their TV screen. Additionally, there were staff members within our program, and coaches from outside of Team Canada, who believed in me and never let me forget it.

Authentic belief from respected people in your life holds a lot of power. Support from my wife, and the safe honesty she provided, was priceless through the ups and downs. Never ending support from my family and friends, regardless of performance, elevated my experience. Finally, interactions with young softball players, in what sometimes seemed like an insignificant moment—whose future you might inspire—was one more aspect of human connection that allowed me to remember how much bigger sport really is than one at bat, one game, or one tournament.

*Jen*: The support you had from friends and family obviously was a booster for you.

How did leadership affect your performance, both yours and those around you/coaches, etc?

*Joey*: The more confident I became as a leader the better I seemed to perform as an athlete. The more I developed as an athlete, the more confident I became as a leader. It is incredible how increasing confidence in one space can spill into and enhance others. I experience this in life too!

For most of my career, I was coached by being told what I was doing wrong and to implement a specific fix. During the final year of my career, the extra year during the pandemic/Olympic delay that wasn't even supposed to happen, I worked with some incredible women at OGX Softball who opened my eyes to a whole new philosophy. These women empowered me to take control of my own development, to learn my own story, to understand my natural tendencies and limitations, and to implement specific drills to enhance my strengths and development. These women gave me a voice and helped me become the best version of myself. My role at the Olympics was to be ready, always. I was an off-the-bench player that summer and I owned that role with confidence: I pinch ran, helped pitchers prepare to go in mid-game, and was in the starting lineup once, going two-for-two with a walk!

Leadership I didn't jive with inspired me to work extremely hard on my mental game in order to hone the ability to own my mentality and experience. Leadership I felt aligned with supported and enhanced that endeavor. The most impactful leadership, in my opinion, occurs with empowerment and collaboration instead of with ego.

*Jen*: It sounds like you learned how to navigate leadership internally really well. To that end, how do factors like the behaviors around Belonging, Resilience, Authenticity, Vulnerability and Empathy (B.R.A.V.E.) directly impact you as a player?

*Joey*: Every B.R.A.V.E. factor impacted me as an athlete and continues to impact me as a coach and human. Resilience is a huge reason I was able to pursue such a long career in sport. A path pursuing goals is never linear; overcoming obstacles is a necessity. Without resilience, giving up would have been the easy answer on many occasions. Empathy allowed me to recognize when a teammate might need a side conversation or a simple sign that I was in their corner as they faced a personal or sport-related battle. Empathy gave us the ability to see new perspectives and to feel seen in an environment that was often relentless.

A sense of belonging elevated my ability to be authentically me and to be vulnerable. As those three factors worked together, our team saw immense improvement in our culture and, ultimately, our performance. Remove these factors from our team's experience and we do not medal at the Olympics. It's that simple.

*Jen*: What a powerful statement! Removing the elements of B.R.A.V.E. from your team performance equates to you not winning a medal on the biggest stage in sports. The importance of these behaviors can't be overstated. So, now that you are no longer playing at that level, how did what you experienced with Team Canada in the Olympics inform the decisions you made regarding your career after the actual playing time was over? What are you doing now that is directly BECAUSE of what you experienced as a pro/Olympic athlete?

***Joey***: The experience I had as an athlete has completely defined this next phase of my life. Because of the struggles I had with imposter syndrome, confidence, and my overall mindset, because of the work that went into shaping a brain that could perform under pressure on the biggest stage, because of the incredible culture we created on that Olympic Team, because of the person I was able to become through sport and the lessons I learned along the way, I have set out to empower women and girls in sports, in business, and in life.

I spent too many years as an athlete, as a woman, trying to be the person I thought others wanted me to be. Doing the work to peel back the layers, discover and show up as my authentic self, and leverage a powerful support system has set me up with a new perspective and purpose to carry forward. I want to give as many women as possible the tools to take control of their own journey and help them create systems of empowerment for themselves and their team, company, or department. We deserve the ability, and the encouragement, to own our story. We deserve to feel valued. We have more than earned our seat at the table. We have so much brilliance to share with the world.

***Jen***: Joey, powerful beyond measure. Thank you for sharing your words with our readers. You are a powerhouse and a gift to the world. I can't wait to work with you again soon!

When I first met Joey, her passion for the game was palpable. In fact, her passion for everything she does can be seen and heard in all aspects. I have no doubt what is next for her will be epic in every way.

The desire for a win, or the need to achieve goals and results both on and off the field isn't lost on me. Some would say I am highly competitive. There is also nothing wrong with that, in the right amounts and the right circumstances. And yet, for so many I have asked along the way, the answer to the question "Why do you play?" has been typically focused on one basic instinct: "Because I love it."

---

**CASE STUDY**

Matt Fields, Former MLB 1st Baseman for multiple teams in the league

---

One of my long-time clients and good friends is a former pro baseball player by the name of Matt Fields. I had the opportunity to watch him grow and thrive not just as a baseball player, but as a human being. And it was he who led me to creating those five-word mantras for the first time when I asked him why he played baseball.

FOR LOVE OF THE GAME. It will be the constant thread that we are bound by as competitors, as people passionate about our pursuits, as lovers of something bigger than ourselves. It will always be the thing that drives us, even in the hardest of moments. There is no question whether or not these factors affect performance. Simply, they do.

*Jen*: Hey, my friend. It's so good to connect again. Tell us about what made you fall in love with your sport and with being an athlete.

*Matt*: Falling in love with a sport often comes from a combination of personal experiences, influences, and role models. For many, it starts in childhood with playing the game, watching it, or being inspired by athletes who embody the spirit of the sport. Ken Griffey, Jr. is a prime example of such a role model. Known for his smooth swing, infectious smile, and genuine love for baseball, Griffey Jr. inspired countless fans, especially those who saw themselves reflected in his journey. His style of play, marked by both grace and power, along with his joy on the field, made baseball not just a game, but an exciting and passionate pursuit. Seeing someone who looks like you succeed and have fun can create a powerful connection to the sport, making it more than just a pastime, but a lifelong passion as it was for me.

*Jen*: What aspects of the human connection made you thrive as a pro athlete?

*Matt*: The aspects of human connection that can make someone thrive as a pro athlete include the bonds formed with teammates, the sense of camaraderie, and the shared goals. Teamwork is essential; it involves trusting and relying on one another, understanding each other's strengths and weaknesses, and working together towards a common objective. Being a leader in this context means more than just performing well, it means inspiring and motivating others, providing support and encouragement, and setting an example both on and off the field.

Being able to pick people up when they are down is a crucial part of this. It fosters a supportive environment where everyone feels valued and empowered to give their best. This mutual support can significantly enhance team performance and individual satisfaction, contributing to a more cohesive and successful group. The connection and trust built through these experiences create a strong foundation that allows athletes to thrive not just as players, but as people.

*Jen*: How did leadership affect your performance, both yours and those around you/coaches, etc.?

*Matt*: Leadership can significantly impact both individual and team performance. Positive leadership can unlock potential and foster an environment where athletes feel free to express themselves and reach their full capabilities. When leadership provides the freedom to be who you are destined to be, it can remove the metaphorical handcuffs, allowing for personal and collective growth.

In your experience, feeling restricted early in your career might have limited your ability to perform at your best. However, once leadership allowed for more freedom and self-expression, you exceeded expectations. Unfortunately, feeling like you don't t have control over your career can be a challenging and demotivating experience, affecting your sense of agency and satisfaction.

For both athletes and coaches, effective leadership involves empowering individuals, providing clear guidance while allowing for autonomy, and creating a supportive environment where everyone can thrive. This balance can lead to enhanced performance, greater fulfillment, and a more cohesive and successful team.

*Jen*: How do factors like the behaviors around Belonging, Resilience, Authenticity, Vulnerability and Empathy (B.R.A.V.E.) directly impact you as a player?

*Matt*: Factors like Belonging, Resilience, Authenticity, Vulnerability, and Empathy (B.R.A.V.E.) have a profound impact on me as a player. Belonging, feling a sense of belonging within a team, provides a foundation of trust and security. It allows me to fully engage and commit to the team's goals, knowing that I am valued and accepted for who I am. This sense of belonging boosts my confidence and fosters a positive mindset, which directly enhances my performance on the field.

Resilience. Resilience is crucial for overcoming setbacks and challenges. Embracing resilience means learning from failures and bouncing back stronger. This mindset helps me maintain focus and determination, even when faced with adversity, ultimately improving my ability to perform under pressure and stay motivated.

Authenticity. Being authentic allows me to play with passion and integrity. When I can be true to myself, my performance becomes more genuine and inspired. Authenticity also builds trust with teammates and coaches, creating an environment where open communication and collaboration can thrive.

Vulnerability. Embracing vulnerability means acknowledging my weaknesses and seeking support when needed. It encourages growth and development by allowing me to learn from others and improve areas where I might struggle. Vulnerability fosters deeper connections with teammates, creating a supportive network that strengthens the overall team dynamic.

Empathy. Empathy enhances my ability to understand and connect with my teammates on a deeper level. It promotes a culture of support and compassion, where everyone feels valued and understood. This connection leads to better teamwork, as we can anticipate each other's needs and provide the necessary support, both on and off the field.

Overall, these B.R.A.V.E. behaviors create an environment that nurtures personal and professional growth. They enable me to perform at my best by fostering a sense of community, encouraging resilience, promoting authenticity, embracing vulnerability, and cultivating empathy. These factors not only enhance individual performance but also contribute to the success and cohesion of the entire team.

*Jen*: How did that inform your career after the actual playing of the game piece was over? Like what are you doing now that directly is BECAUSE of what you experienced as a pro athlete?

*Matt*: The experiences and lessons I gained as a pro athlete have deeply informed and shaped my speaking/teaching career after retiring from the game. Here's how each aspect of my athletic journey has directly influenced my current endeavors:

First, Leadership and Teamwork. The leadership skills I developed and the teamwork I experienced as a player are now central to my career. I work in a role that involves managing and mentoring teams, where I apply the principles of effective leadership and foster a collaborative environment. My ability to inspire, motivate, and support others has been crucial in driving success in my current position.

Second, Resilience and Adaptability. The resilience I built as an athlete, learning to bounce back from setbacks and stay focused under pressure, has been invaluable. In my current career, I face challenges with a determined and adaptable mindset. This resilience has helped me navigate the ups and downs of the professional world, enabling me to stay motivated and achieve my goals.

Next, Authenticity and Vulnerability. Being true to myself and embracing vulnerability on the field has translated into my professional life. I prioritize authenticity in my interactions, fostering genuine connections with colleagues and clients. This has led me to roles where transparency and honesty are valued, and where I can mentor others to embrace their true selves.

Empathy and Support. The empathy I developed as a teammate has become a cornerstone of my current career. I strive to understand and support those I work with, creating an inclusive and compassionate environment. This focus on empathy has enhanced my ability to build strong relationships and effectively collaborate with diverse groups.

Finally, Community Building. The sense of belonging I felt within my team has inspired me to create and nurture communities in my post-athletic career. Whether through professional networks, community outreach, or team projects, I actively work to build environments where everyone feels valued and connected.

Meet Them Where They Are

Overall, my experiences as a pro athlete have directly influenced my current career, driving me to roles that emphasize leadership, resilience, authenticity, vulnerability, and empathy. These principles not only guide my professional actions but also continue to inspire me to create positive, supportive environments where everyone can thrive.

⌒⌣⌒

Matt wasn't just a good baseball player; he is a good motivator. His story has lent itself to inspiring so many young ballplayers yearning for the same pathway as he walked. From the minors, to a luggage handler at the airport and back, Matt has inspired so many to keep their dreams in the palm of their hands—no matter where it leads to.

---

### CASE STUDY

Shannon Boxx, 3x Olympic Gold Medalist, World Cup Champion, National Soccer hall of Fame class of 2022, Entrepreneur, keynote speaker and TV Sports Analyst.

---

I had the good fortune to work with another inspirational person, Olympian and former US Women's National Soccer Team Hall of Famer, Shannon Boxx. I spent some time with her helping to create a model that would help female athletes as they transitioned out of their sport and into their next career. She has successfully taken that to market and is working with both pro and collegiate athletes who are looking toward their next adventure. She is a rockstar of epic proportions. Her care and compassion for her teammates, her friends, and her family are easy to see and feel. She is a Hall of Famer for so many reasons. Here is our conversation around performance and how B.R.A.V.E. Human Leadership plays a role

*Jen*: Shannon, as always, it's great to connect. You have had an incredible career as a very accomplished athlete. Tell us about what made you fall in love with soccer.

*Shannon*: As a youth player my "why" was simple. I played sports because I loved to compete. Sports empowered me to dream without limits. On the playing field gender norms didn't apply. Out on the playing field I loved that I could showcase my strength, my competitiveness, and my toughness. Soccer specifically became my favorite because I love how creative and strategic it is. The game not only requires physical skill and agility, but it also requires mental skills and quick thinking.

*Jen*: Along the lines of those less tangible skills, what aspects of the human connection do you think made you thrive as an Olympic/pro athlete?

*Shannon*: One aspect that I loved about a team sport was the connection between my teammates and myself. Great teams exist as one unit. They trust each other, they push each other, and they support each other. I thrived on the national team because we shared a winning mentality and a collective goal and every single game, and every training we focused on ourselves and set this high standard for each other. We knew if everyone played their role to the best of their ability, we all won.

*Jen*: Because of that high collective standard, how do you feel leadership affected your performance—both yours and those around you, your coaches, etc.?

*Shannon*: I have always believed the best leaders are those that lead by example. When you have leaders who put the team first above all else, they can help create a winning culture. Building a culture that is cohesive and values the collective spirit can only be achieved by the people within that culture.

*Jen*: How do factors like the behaviors around Belonging, Resilience, Authenticity, Vulnerability and Empathy (B.R.A.V.E.) directly impact you as a player?

*Shannon*: So, if I think about belonging, I think the more connected you are to each of your teammates, then it just makes the game that much easier, right? So, I just think connection is the first step to having the right culture and the feeling of belonging to be able to play together effectively. After all, it's a team sport and each of its players has a role to play.

And so, anyone playing a sport knows, you will win sometimes and you will lose sometimes and the critical piece is that you have to learn how to be resilient, to be able to not let the failures stop you from fulfilling a goal or a dream. For so many reasons, resilience has been my superpower. I would just say that I look back at my path to excellence and I can recognize it was never straight, and I felt like my ability to continue to push forward despite the odds against me was strong. I still did what I had to even when it was hard because I had this unwavering ability to just continue to believe in myself.

As far as authenticity, I truly believe you really can't get far unless you're being who you really are. I had this conversation with my daughter earlier: if you're playing for somebody else because other people tell you you should or somebody else wants something, you're never going to be able to continue to work hard at it. So, I think that if you're not truly being your authentic self when you're playing a sport, eventually you're not going to be able to get through the hard times because you will be doing it for the wrong reasons.

At some point you're not going to go out and do the extra work that you need to, because it really isn't about you, it's about doing it for your parents. But if it's something you want, it's your dream and your goal, you're going to do the extra things because it's something you enjoy doing and you love it. It's a lot easier to achieve something hard when you love it authentically.

For me, that connection beforehand is so much more about trust … and so I think the greater teams are the ones that can trust each other. You know, you look at this current U.S. Women's National team that just won. The big difference from the year before and this year is that they trusted each other to be able to be themselves out there, where I don't think they trusted that as much last year, that they could be themselves and play freely. So much of it has to do with a solid trust in their coach. You could see how it allowed them to play together a lot better and with more synergy. And empathy for me … I mean, I just think that's just being a good human.

Obviously, you know people go through hard times, and I don't think it's super hard to bring empathy to that just as a human, even when you are competitive. The standup athletes in my mind are the ones that can be super competitive, but do it in a way that's morally in the right space. Those are the athletes that I want to compete with. You can be competitive, even a little aggressive and want to win, but not at all costs.

As an example, Brazil beat us in 2007, and it was the worst display of sportsmanship I remember seeing from an opponent. After they won, they threw it in our faces. It felt pretty bad. I couldn't understand why they weren't more empathetic. We had beaten them every single big event besides this one and we had never done that.

Even in 2011, when we lost to Japan, I was so bummed because I'm a competitor. However, there was a part of me that understood and knew … and maybe it was more to save myself … in the end, they might have needed this more than we needed this. That win was right after the tsunami. I respected them as a team and so I was empathetic to feel like obviously as a competitor I wish we won and I wanted to win, but as a human being, I knew how much this win meant to them. I was able to go over to one of my great friends on the Japanese team and congratulate her because I felt that deeply. I think there is something great about creating empathetic competition. It's about seeing the human side and remembering that it exists no matter what happens.

***Jen***: How did all of that inform your career after you started down the path of retirement? What are you doing now that directly is BECAUSE of what you experienced as a pro/Olympic athlete?

***Shannon***: What I am doing now is directly related to what I experienced in my own transition away from sports. Going from knowing exactly who you are and what you want, to asking yourself what's next is a scary place to be. I struggled with the loss of my identity, my team, and my purpose and I felt my worth was tied to what I had accomplished. Through my journey I realized there wasn't enough being done to support and assist female athletes to position them to succeed beyond their sport. So, I created Athletes Redefined, a program that supports and empowers athletes to find or create their own authentic path and equip them with the tools necessary for a successful and fulfilling life both during and after their sport.

Shannon has been an inspiration to so many and her story is a beacon of hope for so many who are making a big change in their lives, changing careers or just trying to figure out what is next.

---

## CASE STUDY

Vince Malts, Former NHL player, Owner of Bloodline Hockey, certified USA Hockey Level 4 Coach, and first Mindset and Performance Coach in the NHL.

---

I met Vince Malts about 12 years ago when we were both in a mastermind group for people doing similar work. We wanted to help others become the best versions of themselves and so we knew we needed to be the best versions of ourselves first. We joined this virtual group at the same time and got to know each other, becoming friends along the way. Vince is a former pro hockey player in the NHL, a hockey coach, and the first mindset and performance coach in the NHL.

*Jen*: What made you fall in love with hockey?

*Vince*: Initially, I think it was the raw energy of the game that drew me in. Hockey challenged every part of my physical nature and spirit. I loved going as hard as I possibly could, and the game was designed with that same intense spirit in mind, especially back when I was coming up in it. I had all this explosive, non-stop energy that needed an outlet, and hockey was the perfect match. It let me express who I naturally was as a human being.

I think that's what first made me fall in love with it—just how naturally it aligned with who I was, both physically and emotionally. It gave me a place to channel all that energy in a healthy way (well, most of the time), and it helped shape my spirit and personality.

And, of course, as a kid, sometimes it was as simple as the joy of scoring goals. I remember how amazing it felt. Scoring was the best feeling in the world. I loved to compete. Whether it was a race to the goal line or a game-winning shot, I wanted to win every single time. I wanted to score, and then I wanted to score more. Those experiences created a deep, lasting love for the game at an early age.

Another big part of it was just the simple pleasure of playing outside with neighborhood kids—roller hockey or street hockey for hours. No pressure, no commitments, just pure fun. Even though high-level hockey came with challenges and commitments, I think having that outlet—where I'd spend six to eight hours a day just playing for the love of it—was crucial. There wasn't any pressure like you'd feel in a game or a practice. It was just playing outside, hanging out with friends, and enjoying the game. That was another huge aspect of what deepened my love for hockey.

Free play was where I could really immerse myself in the game. Playing with AAA teams limited how many practices or games I could have each week, but with street and roller hockey, I could just keep going. It felt like an infinite game: an endless pursuit of joy and creativity with no end in sight. It was different from the structured practices and games where everything was more finite. Playing with friends in the street gave me that infinite feeling, and I think that's what truly drove my passion and love for the game. It kept hockey alive for me, even when I wasn't on the ice.

***Jen***: Along the lines of the less tangible skills, what aspects of the human connection do you think made you thrive as a pro athlete?

***Vince***: When I think about what aspects of human connection helped me thrive as a pro athlete, it's definitely the veteran leadership on the team. One particular season comes to mind when I played with

Nathan Lutz, Rod Aldoff, and Cory Laylin. That year, their leadership was everything to me.

Rod, Cory, and Nathan had been in the game for a long time, and they shared so much wisdom with me. I was young and full of energy—maybe even a little too emotional at times—and they really helped ground me. They brought peace of mind, making me realize that I wasn't crazy for feeling how I felt. They helped me see the game from a different perspective, teaching me how to understand it like a true professional.

Each one of them had a different style, too. Rod was more of the "let's sit down, have a coffee, and talk it out" type. Cory, on the other hand, would share wisdom during warm-ups. We'd go through our pre-game routine, and those small moments turned into valuable lessons that stuck with me. And Nathan, he was my buddy: someone my age who already had a great foundation of what true leadership meant. We'd hang out, work out together, and he just had this natural leadership quality. He eventually became the captain of the team and was someone I really looked up to.

So, for me, the human connection that helped me thrive as a pro came down to the veteran leadership in the room. I gravitated towards those players, and their influence made a massive impact on me—not just as an athlete, but as a person.

*Jen*: How do you feel leadership affected your performance – both yours and those around you, your coaches, etc.?

*Vince*: Leadership had a huge impact, not just on my own performance, but on the entire team. I've experienced both ends of the spectrum: the negative, almost toxic side, and the positive, supportive side. One season, I played under a coach who, honestly, every single guy on the team just couldn't stand. I remember defending him a few times, saying, "He's not that bad," or "He's actually a good guy," and I'd get attacked for it because of how strongly the guys felt against him. They just hated him, and it was crazy to see how that really impacted our performance.

The atmosphere was so hostile that any chance the team got to push back against this coach, they took it. I saw it firsthand, especially when we hit the playoffs. I watched our team basically throw in the towel on this coach. We were in a position to make a run, but they were like, "Nope, we're done. We're not playing for you anymore." It was sad to see because, at the end of the day, we're all professionals, but the coach's poor leadership—his demeaning, yelling, treating us like kids—just eroded all trust and motivation.

On the flip side, when I played for a coach who actually cared—one who let us play our game—the energy was completely different. The team stayed even-keeled; there was this consistent, calm energy because we knew what to expect. There weren't any surprises, and we felt supported, which made a massive difference in how we performed on the ice. It's amazing how a coach's energy can impact the entire locker room. When you trust your leader, it frees you up to play with confidence and authenticity.

That's the thing about leadership: there's an authority bias in all of us. Either you trust the person leading you and feel like they have your back, or you don't. When you don't believe the leader cares, you get tense, and you start doing things out of character just to stay on their good side. The best leaders allow you to be who you are instead of trying to mold you into what they think is best. They understand the team's chemistry and respect that, instead of imposing their own ego-driven ideas.

So yeah, leadership really did affect my performance and the team's. It's the difference between thriving and just surviving.

*Jen*: How have factors like the behaviors around Belonging, Resilience, Authenticity, Vulnerability, and Empathy (B.R.A.V.E.) directly impacted you as a player and coach?

*Vince*: Belonging plays such a crucial role, both as a player and a coach. I had an experience with two different departments in one organization that really highlighted this for me. In one department, I felt like I truly belonged. The leader made me feel valued, inspired me, and believed in my ideas. Under that leadership, I was confident and able to contribute in ways that aligned with the department's needs. I produced great work because I felt empowered to bring my best self forward.

But in another department, it was the complete opposite. The leader constantly made me feel like I was beneath him, like I didn't have the intellectual capacity to keep up. He always made sure I knew my place, and that kind of leadership restricted me. It was uncomfortable and demoralizing. I was hesitant to share my thoughts, and it killed any desire I had to contribute in a meaningful way. So, experiencing both sides of belonging taught me just how important it is: when you belong, you thrive; when you don't, you shut down.

As a player, belonging mattered just as much. When I was on teams where I felt like a first-line guy, I felt incredible. I wanted to give everything I had to the team. But when I was on third or fourth lines, just sent out to fight or throw big hits, I didn't feel like I belonged in the same way. That feeling of being valued—of having a role that mattered—was missing, and it affected my mindset. I see the same thing with young players today. The stars of the team get a lot of love and attention, which builds their confidence, while the third or fourth-line guys don't get the same feeling of belonging, and it shows in their performance.

Resilience, for me, was something I only really learned as I got older. I knew it was important, but I didn't fully grasp what healthy resilience looked like until later in my career. In my younger days, I'd react too quickly, sending emails I shouldn't have or saying things in the heat of the moment. As I matured, I learned that resilience meant knowing when to hold back, when to take a breath, and when to approach situations more thoughtfully. I learned that it's about resisting the urge to act impulsively, whether that's judging a coach or a teammate without fully understanding their perspective. Emotional resilience became about waiting for the right time to have those conversations, aligning myself with others first, and approaching everything with more patience.

Authenticity is another rare but powerful factor. As a player, I didn't encounter many authentic coaches. There was one, though: Jack Capuano. Jack didn't always tell you everything, but his energy was real. He was laid-back and honest, and you knew exactly where you stood with him. When Jack came in after a particularly challenging coach was let go, his authenticity allowed the team to just play freely. You could feel it in the room. The authenticity he brought made everyone more comfortable and it translated to success on the ice.

For me, as a coach, I became more authentic after my daughter was born. I remember coaching a U18 team, and as I watched the players skate, I had this realization that every one of them was someone's kid. It hit me in a way that completely shifted my approach. Before, I was extremely demanding. Ninety to 95% of my coaching style was about pushing players hard. But after that moment, I realized there was another side to coaching. I became more laid-back, more matter-of-fact, and more focused on helping players see the bigger picture. My coaching shifted to about 90% being calm and real with them, and 5 to 10% pushing them when they really needed it. That balance brought out my authentic self, and I think the players responded better because of it.

Vulnerability is one of the hardest things for male athletes and coaches, especially in the pro world. There's this cultural bias: this idea that showing emotion or opening up isn't "cool." It's not something that comes naturally to male performers, and it's even tougher when you're working under leaders who don't want to hear about how you feel. I've seen players try to be vulnerable with their coaches in private, only to have that coach use it against them in front of the team later during video sessions, or team meetings. That breaks trust instantly, and it shuts down any chance of creating a culture where vulnerability is encouraged.

It's such a delicate balance because vulnerability requires trust, and once that trust is broken, it's hard to rebuild. It takes a special kind of leader to nurture that vulnerability and create a space where players and coaches feel safe to open up. But when it works, it creates a stronger, more connected team culture.

Lastly, empathy. This is truly a superpower in today's game and life in general. As a mindset and performance coach, I've learned that empathy is essential. It's about putting yourself in someone else's shoes, whether it's a player, a staff member, a parent, or anyone in your world. It's a team game, and if you can consciously recognize how others might be seeing a situation, you solve problems more effectively.

Empathy slows your mind down and stops you from rushing to fix things immediately. Instead of thinking you have to solve everything right away, empathy teaches you to gather more data, consider all perspectives, and then work toward a solution that benefits everyone. It's the difference between "me" and "we," and the leaders who understand that are the ones who build the strongest teams. They're not just focused on their own perspective—they're actively considering how everyone else is thinking and feeling, and that leads to healthier, more productive outcomes.

***Jen***: How did all of that inform your career after you started down the path of retirement? What are you doing now that directly is BECAUSE of what you experienced as a pro athlete?

***Vince***: After going through all the experiences I had during my career, I realized they directly led me to what I do now as a mental performance coach. It all started when I retired and knew I wanted to get into coaching, but I didn't want to just teach players the technical side of the game. I felt a strong pull to educate them on what it truly means to be a professional human being—to develop a professional mindset and understand the cultural process behind it.

One of the biggest turning points for me was when I got injured early in my career, right after being drafted by the Vancouver Canucks. I didn't have anyone to support me or guide me through that critical period. There was no one to tell me, "Hey, this is normal. You got injured, and it's going to set you back a bit, but it's part of the process." I didn't have someone to explain that it would take years to develop fully as a professional—that it's a long journey and nothing to be discouraged about.

I'll never forget the first time I went back to Vancouver's training camp after that injury. I was put on a line with Mark Messier, and I remember thinking, "*What am I doing out here? I don't belong here.*" My self-esteem was low, and I felt completely out of place. If someone had been there to say, "It's going to take a few years to find your rhythm again, and that's okay. This is what young pros go through," it would have made a world of difference. I didn't have that voice of reason, and I had no one to help me understand that professional growth is a long-term process.

These experiences taught me the value of having someone there to help you navigate those challenging times. It wasn't until years later that I fully realized how much I needed that guidance: someone to help me avoid self-sabotage and impatience, to not react impulsively or burn bridges with leaders who weren't a good fit. I didn't know how to be patient with myself, and I was always in a rush, feeling like everything had to happen immediately.

That's why, when I work with players now, I focus on normalizing their experiences and helping them see that what they're going through is part of the process. Whether it's a rough patch or struggling to understand their role on the team, I try to show them that these feelings are normal and to be expected. I help them develop habits around consistency, simplicity, and clear communication, whether it's with their coaches, GMs, or families. It's about building that rhythm, having meaningful dialogue, and making sure they have a strategy to navigate all the challenges that come their way.

My experience also made me see the importance of recognizing the narratives we create in our heads. Are you feeling like you're not being utilized enough? Do you feel overlooked? I help players articulate these thoughts and share them in productive ways. I encourage them to have real conversations, align themselves with the team, and become peaceful within the chaos that is professional sports. That's something I didn't have as a young player, and it's exactly what I want to give back now.

Becoming a mental performance coach, especially the first mindset and performance coach in the NHL, came directly from everything I went through. From my injury to dealing with poor leadership, to making mistakes as a young coach, I realized I needed to develop the skills to communicate these lessons to others. I love being able to help players and coaches understand the patience, perspective, and strategies they need to succeed.

It's about helping them create peace of mind amid the chaos. I find that the brain craves strategy; it wants to make sense of things in patterns. So, when you can align yourself with those natural patterns, it brings a calmness that helps you perform at your best. Every single challenge I faced as a player and coach, and all the mistakes I made, have equipped me to now contribute in what I believe is a meaningful way to today's players, coaches, and leaders.

That's why I do what I do. It's all because of those experiences. Now I can give back to the ecosystem and culture of the game, supporting the players and leaders coming up today, and that's what's truly fulfilling for me.

---

These five well-accomplished athletes and standout human beings have another thing in common. They all happen to be fantastic inspirational speakers, coaches, and teachers. Examples of top-level athletes and the importance of understanding performance within the concept of B.R.A.V.E. is clear. As you can see with each of them, there was a passion and a love for something greater than themselves. All good leaders need to have this in place as they set out to transform the landscape and the experience of the people around them. They only found the ability to win by leaning into the team of people with whom they surround themselves.

A true champion builds bridges. They empower, listen, and are consistent in their effort and attitude. They also lead by example. And just like the five relational leaders above, the most important thing we can know about them is they aren't just a champion among the team, they are a champion OF the team.

## CHAPTER 16

# How B.R.A.V.E. Is Your Culture?

Businesses of all shapes and sizes are standing on the edge of a new frontier. Only one in three employees is at all engaged per Gallup's 2024 State of the Global Workplace.[1] The study states that, "most employees are not engaged (62%) — those who show up, do the bare minimum and are uninspired by their work — or actively disengaged (15%) — those who have a bad manager and a miserable job and are actively seeking a new one".[2] The total cost of the loss in productivity of those who are not engaged is $8.9 Trillion world-wide.[3] Because of this, leadership is feeling the pressure of a volatile economy, and every business needs to decide how to navigate an AI-driven technological revolution. The stakes have never been higher. How will your organization rise to the challenge?

As the wheels of commerce turn, the US Surgeon General has once again called attention to the public health crisis that loneliness poses for many of us.[2] We're more disconnected than ever, and that shows up in our digital-forward businesses. Bridging the gap between humans and technology poses a unique challenge. Yet, it's only by turning to our people that we can achieve better business outcomes. Employees who feel seen, heard, and valued are more productive. We already know this.

Business leaders and the employees they're responsible for need a pathway to thrive in these extraordinary circumstances. However, if we focus too much of our energy on results and outcomes to drive the bottom line, how do our people feel taken care of? I often ask the large corporations that are very results-driven this simple question: "At what cost?"

These companies were the same ones who were struggling mightily during the "Great Resignation" and "Quiet Quitting" surges that we witnessed over the past few years.

This proves that there has to be a balance between the drive for performance and the care of people. We CAN do both. According to what we have found, most leaders just need to learn how.

Through genuine connection and understanding the why behind your team's goals and desires, this balanced approach proves that high performance does not have to come at the expense of a supportive culture; rather, it thrives because of it.

WHAT OUR RESEARCH HAS SHOWN:

In order to understand the four very clear leader segments that came out of our research more fully, we laid out the descriptions below so that you can practice becoming aware and then shifting behaviors when necessary going forward. After really diving into the data, **one really important piece we recognized right away:**

**Your starting point is not your final destination.**

As you read the descriptions of each segment below, carefully consider which one sounds the most like you. Pay close attention every time we mention that leader segment; we'll provide actionable strategies for your ongoing growth. We know you want to be as successful of a leader as you can be.

**Yearning for More Organizational Support**

The first segment we called Constrained Leaders (32%) and they feel like islands in their organizations and lack the support they feel they need to succeed. Whether they've been leaders for many years or are new to the role, their leadership methods are based on authority, influence, and command rather than mutual connection. With an open heart and mind, they can learn the skills to become Relational Leaders.

What makes this segment distinct is the respondents' agreement with the following statements:

- A strong leader needs to maintain authority over others to be effective.
- I always know what the people I lead are thinking and feeling.
- A strong leader has to be willing to make people uncomfortable to ensure good outcomes for the organization.
- I wish I had more support from my organization in becoming a strong leader.
- Sometimes leaders have to use psychological tricks to get the people they lead to do what they want them to do.
- Because of how my organization functions, I am limited in what I can achieve as a leader.
- It's hard for me to admit my shortcomings as a leader.
- I'm afraid to be vulnerable with the people I lead.

- I struggle to understand what the people I lead want or need from me.
- Sometimes you have to scare the people you lead so they'll work harder.

**Unifying Organizations Through Strong Relationships**

On the other end of the leadership spectrum are the Relational Leaders (19%) segment. These leaders believe their success as leaders hinges on developing positive relationships with those they lead. Their perspective is systems-based and community-oriented, and they believe organizations are responsible for developing effective leaders through their learning and development programs and cultures. These people are typically more focused on balancing people and performance for the best outcomes overall.

Though other segments also agree with some of the sentiments that represent this one, Relational Leaders show stronger agreement with the following:

- Leaders need to be good with people to be effective at their job.
- A leader can only be effective if they build positive relationships with the people they lead.
- Organizations are responsible for creating the right conditions for leaders to be successful.
- Current leaders in my organization demonstrate the qualities I think are important in a leader.
- Being a leader is one of the best ways to contribute to the world in a positive way.
- I model my leadership style after another leader I know.

## Empathetic and Curious About People

Emotionally-Oriented Leaders (23%) are dedicated to their leadership of others and are curious how those they lead view them. They believe empathy is essential for leadership and lead with feeling. They can build more confidence in themselves to become truly Relational Leaders.

While the other segments agree with many of the attitudes that make these empathetic leaders who they are, these professionals strongly agree with these statements:

- I'm determined to become the best leader I can be.
- I can honestly say I care deeply about the people I lead.
- Leaders have to be able to empathize with the people they lead to do a good job.
- My approach to leadership is different from other leaders in my organization.
- I spend a lot of time thinking about the kind of leader I want to be.
- I'm doing my best in my leadership role until I can develop more skills.
- I'm curious about what people I lead think about my leadership qualities.
- With the right training, anybody can become an effective leader.
- Anybody can learn how to be more empathetic.

## Prioritizing Productivity Over All Else

Outcome-Oriented Leaders (26%) focus primarily on productivity and believe they are successful because they effectively drive high performance among those they lead. Reaching the next leadership level requires a more relational approach (and embracing the vulnerability they don't think they need).

These leaders show strong agreement with the following sentiments:

- I know exactly what I need to work on to become a more effective leader.
- Some people are born to be strong leaders.
- I'm one of the best leaders in my organization.
- A leader cannot succeed in an organization without a strong leadership culture to support their efforts.
- The most important thing a leader does is increase the productivity of the people they lead.
- I don't need to be vulnerable to be an effective leader for my organization.

**The State of Leadership Mindsets**

Despite the many differences between the segments outlined above, they all share many attitudes, showing us we're not so different after all. These common attitudes show us that leadership development is shifting toward a more emotionally aware, community-oriented approach.

Most leaders strongly believe their organizations have a **strong leadership culture** and develop leaders well. Consequently, their organizations are sought-after places to work. Leaders also believe their expertise makes them effective and that any leader needs **extensive industry experience** to lead people in their organizations. Leaders' attitudes show us that there's a lot of nuance in what it takes to be a leader. While most leaders strongly believe there are multiple ways to be effective, they also believe there are **specific skills everybody in a leadership role needs to master**. They also believe there's **a lot more to effective leadership than empathizing with the people they lead**. Even the Emotionally-Oriented Leaders, who rest their hats on empathy, strongly agree with this statement. Nonetheless, most strongly agree that a leader should be the **most emotionally intelligent person in the room**; leaders understand awareness is vital to their role.

Most strongly agree that **leadership is a calling**; they think the best leaders think of leadership as who they are, not just a job they do. We were thrilled to see that most strongly agree they want to be part of a **community of industry leaders**. Now more than ever, leaders need to commiserate and collaborate to be most effective in their roles. Leaders also show mild to moderate agreement that **different genders** bring different levels of empathy to leadership.

**Leadership Mindset Comes From Within**

Although you may have ideas about what type of leader is Constrained, Relational, Emotionally-Oriented, or Outcome-Oriented, no demographic or organizational characteristics affect what segment a leader comes from. We've discovered that most (88%) leaders were promoted to leadership from within their organization. That's why it's extra important to cultivate a strong leadership culture in your organization—it fuels strong leaders for years to come.

Over half of the leaders surveyed have been in their current roles for 4-10 years. If we're considering Relational Leaders as the segment that's found the balance between strategic thinking and emotional intelligence, that leaves over three in four leaders with ongoing leadership development needs. The good news:

*WE'VE GOT YOU. This is what we do.*

Here's a way to take a step toward becoming a more relational leader:

**A Practical Guide: Balancing Professional Authority with Personal Vulnerability**

The Vulnerability-Authority Balance Process will help you create a balanced leadership approach that leverages both professional authority and personal vulnerability, fostering trust, openness, and high performance within the team.

- **Reflect on Your Leadership Style**
  - Assess your current approach.
  - Identify areas needing balance.
  - Understand the impact on team dynamics.

  *Timeframe: 1 week.*

- **Cultivate Emotional Intelligence**
  - Develop self-awareness.
  - Practice empathy.
  - Enhance communication skills.

  *Timeframe: Ongoing.*

- **Communicate Openly and Transparently**
  - Share your vulnerabilities.
  - Discuss challenges openly.
  *Timeframe: 2-3 weeks.*

- **Listen to Your Team Members**
  - Actively listen.
  - Value their input.
  *Timeframe: Continuous.*

- **Be Approachable and Accessible**
  - Encourage open-door policies.
  - Be responsive.
  *Timeframe: Continuous.*

- **Delegate and Empower**
  - Trust your team's abilities.
  - Foster autonomy.
  *Timeframe: Ongoing.*

- **Encourage Growth and Development**
  - Provide learning opportunities.
  - Offer feedback constructively.
  *Timeframe: Ongoing.*

## Evaluation

Set regular check-ins (e.g., monthly) to assess progress towards creating a balanced environment where professional authority complements personal vulnerability based upon the deepening of trust and respect.

## Success Indicators

- Enhanced trust within the team.
- Increased openness in communication.

- Greater cohesion and performance among team members.

By integrating these steps into your leadership practice, you can create an environment that not only values, but thrives on vulnerability and authenticity, unlocking unprecedented levels of human potential within your team.

To translate these insights into action, start by conducting regular check-ins with your team members—not just about projects but about their personal well-being and professional aspirations. Implement training sessions that not only focus on skill development but also on emotional intelligence and interpersonal dynamics. Encourage open dialogue where vulnerability is viewed as a pathway to growth rather than a weakness.

Connection and community will come from leading with B.R.A.V.E. Human Leadership at the core of how we show up every day. It is my belief that the more of these behaviors we build and practice, the more we will find our way back to each other in a kinder, more loving way. The stronger communities we will build, naturally, the more connection we will feel. And at the end of the day, success will always be dependent upon this simple equation.

While this book provides a comprehensive guide, it is by no means exhaustive. The landscape of human behavior and organizational psychology is ever-evolving, suggesting areas for further research such as deeper dives into cultural impacts on B.R.A.V.E. behaviors or greater longitudinal studies measuring long-term impacts of these practices in diverse industries.

I urge you to take bold steps toward a more B.R.A.V.E. culture and becoming a true B.R.A.V.E. Leader who can support that culture. Experiment with these principles, adapt them to your unique context, and observe the transformation within your team's dynamics and their outcomes. Let this not be an end, but a beginning to continuously striving towards mastering these behaviors, cultivating an environment where people truly feel a part of something greater than themselves.

*We can do this.*
*We NEED to do this.*

B.R.A.V.E. behaviors are no longer a "nice to have." They are a "need to have" in every scenario where human beings are involved. Oh, and by the way ... Going back to that day in May of 2012, when I was sitting in the stifling hot cab of the moving truck and heard these words:

*"We don't want anything too touchy-feely.*
*Our people aren't really like that."*

Those same 13 words that changed my life. I want you to know, I only tweaked that keynote a little bit. I kept all the stuff that made me, well ... ME. I talked about the need for connection and community and how empathy just makes us better humans. Linda ran up to me at the end and gave me a hug and said what I have heard hundreds, maybe thousands of times since then:

**"That was EXACTLY what we needed."**

**Warning:** *People ARE touchy-feely.* To ignore that fact is to miss the greatest asset we will ever have at our disposal. This is the moment where influence for good becomes our legacy. Where we can be heart-centered AND performance focused.

Where we have the ability to bring people together to solve the loneliness crisis, to mend the many divides we feel around us on a daily basis, and to allow our differences to actually be our strengths, not our weaknesses. Where we can lead from a place of understanding, not try to motivate by fear and reprimand. Perhaps THIS is exactly what we need.

Welcome to a different conversation on leadership, where we are building community and connection with intention. This is the conversation we need to be having authentically, not only to save our families and our workplaces, but to save our humanity at the very core.

Every single one of us plays a role in this work. We have an obligation to each other and to ourselves to find the common thread of which we all hold a piece.

A few years before my dad died, he handed me a white piece of paper with some typed words on it and told me he thought of me when he read it. He told me to take it and read it when I got home and then hugged me goodbye. I opened it later that night when I was getting changed for bed. It was a quote that I have felt so deeply from that day forward:

> *"Do not be daunted by the enormity of the world's grief.*
> *Do justly now, love mercy now, walk humbly now.*
> *You are not obligated to complete the work,*
> *but neither are you free to abandon it".*[5]

So be it, and so it is. May we all pledge to continue the work to see and hold the thread that witnesses the very humanity in each of us.

*And may we be B.R.A.V.E. enough to meet each other where we are.*

# ENDNOTES

Chapter 2

1. Brown, B. (2020). *The gifts of imperfection*. Random House.
2. Martino, J., Pegg, J., & Frates, E. P. (2015). The connection prescription: Using the power of social interactions and the deep desire for connectedness to empower health and Wellness. *American Journal of Lifestyle Medicine, 11*(6), 466–475. https://doi.org/10.1177/1559827615608788
3. Martino, J., Pegg, J., & Frates, E. P. (2015). The connection prescription: Using the power of social interactions and the deep desire for connectedness to empower health and Wellness. *American Journal of Lifestyle Medicine, 11*(6), 466–475. https://doi.org/10.1177/1559827615608788
4. Holt-lunstad, J., & Smith, T. (2010). Social relationships and mortality risk: A metaanalytic review. *SciVee*. https://doi.org/10.4016/19911.01
5. Holt-lunstad, J., & Smith, T. (2010). Social relationships and mortality risk: A metaanalytic review. *SciVee*. https://doi.org/10.4016/19911.01

6. Holt-lunstad, J., & Smith, T. (2010). Social relationships and mortality risk: A metaanalytic review. *SciVee*. https://doi.org/10.4016/19911.01

7. Pinker, S. (2014a). *The village effect*. Atlantic Books.

8. *Connect with others*. Mental Health America. (n.d.). https://www.mhanational.org/connect-others

## Chapter 4

1. Robertson, D. D. and A. (2023, December 18). *Reversing the customer trust deficit*. Gallup.com. https://www.gallup.com/workplace/470618/reversing-customer-trust-deficit.aspx

2. Robertson, D. D. and A. (2023, December 18). *Reversing the customer trust deficit*. Gallup.com. https://www.gallup.com/workplace/470618/reversing-customer-trust-deficit.aspx

3. Hickman, A. (2023, July 21). *Talk (a lot) about your company's culture change*. Gallup.com. https://www.gallup.com/workplace/284036/talk-lot-company-culture-change.aspx#:~:text=Gallup%20research%20reveals%20that%20less,opportunity%20t%20get%20to%20work.

4. Economy, P. (2019, January 15). The (millennial) workplace of the future is almost here -- these 3 things are about to change Big time | inc.com. https://www.inc.com/peter-economy/the-millennial-workplace-of-future-is-almost-here-these-3-things-are-about-tochange-big-time.html

5. Bradshaw, R. (2024, June 7). *17 remarkable career change statistics to know (2024)*. Apollo Technical LLC. https://www.apollotechnical.com/career-change-statistics/

6. Wigert, B. (2023, July 21). *Employee burnout: The biggest myth*. Gallup.com. https://www.gallup.com/workplace/288539/employee-burnout-biggest-myth.aspx

7. Harvard Business School (HBS) Working Knowledge. (2015, February 2). *Workplace stress responsible for up to $190B in annual U.S. Healthcare Costs.* Forbes. https://www.forbes.com/sites/hbsworkingknowledge/2015/01/26/workplace-stressresponsible-for-up-to-190-billion-in-annual-u-s-heathcare-costs/

8. Work-life balance. OECD Better Life Index. (n.d.). https://www.oecdbetterlifeindex.org/topics/work-life-balance/#:~:text=In%20Italy%2C%20full%2Dtime%20workers,OECD%20average%20f%2015%20hours.

9. Work-life balance. OECD Better Life Index. (n.d.). https://www.oecdbetterlifeindex.org/topics/work-life-balance/#:~:text=In%20Italy%2C%20full%2Dtime%20workers,OECD%20average%20of%2015%20hours.

## Chapter 5

1. Oxford English Dictionary. (n.d.). https://www.oed.com/

2. Robison, B. W. and J. (2024, March 20). *Fostering creativity at work: Do your managers push or Crush Innovation?.* Gallup.com. https://www.gallup.com/workplace/245498/fostering-creativity-work-managers-pushcrush-innovation.aspx

3. Robison, B. W. and J. (2024, March 20). Fostering creativity at work: Do your managers push or Crush Innovation?. Gallup.com. https://www.gallup.com/workplace/245498/fostering-creativity-work-managers-pushcrush-innovation.aspx

4. Leadership Success. (2024, February 13). Lewins Leadership Style: Kurt Lewin Leadership styles. Lewins Leadership Style | Kurt Lewin Leadership Styles. https://www.leadershipsuccess.co/leadership-styles/lewins-leadership-styles#:~:text=In%20

1939%2C%20social%20psychology%2C%20Kurt,how%20a%20eader%20makes%20decisions.

5. *Defining tra*nsactional leadership. Western Governors University. (2022, October 24). https://www.wgu.edu/blog/transactional-leadership2103.html#:~:text=The%20roots%20of%20transactional%20leadership,woul%20eventually%20become%20transactional%20leadership.

6. What is transformational leadership? A model for motivating innovation. CIO. (2024, July 15). https://www.cio.com/article/228465/what-is-transformational-leadership-a-model-for-motivating-innovation.html#:~:text=The%20concept%20of%20transformational%20leadership,the%20success%20of%20transformational%20leadership.

## Chapter 6

1. Nicioli, T. (2023, October 24). *The loneliness epidemic: Nearly 1 in 4 adults feel lonely, new survey finds.* CNN. https://www.cnn.com/2023/10/24/health/lonely-adults-gallup-poll-wellness/index.html

## Chapter 7

1. Williams, M. (1958). The velveteen rabbit. Heinemann Young Books.

2. Williams, M. (1958). The velveteen rabbit. Heinemann Young Books.

3. Tsukamoto, F. (2020b, September 14). *Kintsugi (金継ぎ) - the art of f*ixing broken pottery and reuse. Abokichi. https://www.abokichi.com/blogs/news/kintsugi-the-art-to-fix-broken-pottery-and-reuse?gad_source=1&gclid=CjwKCAjwko21BhAPEiwAwfaQCPdmX6TDpxD8WHJhG_W-AtpHRxyt7AE_akBKfJEM2Q-Dm2aJ0Dx4DhoC1a8QAvD_BwE

Chapter 8

1. Audience Audit, & Human Leadership Institute. (2024, September). How B.R.A.V.E. Human Leadership Behaviors Define Relational Leaders: Leading With Mind and Heart. https://www.thehli.com/research/

2. Audience Audit, & Human Leadership Institute. (2024, September). How B.R.A.V.E. Human Leadership Behaviors Define Relational Leaders: Leading With Mind and Heart. https://www.thehli.com/research/

3. Audience Audit, & Human Leadership Institute. (2024, September). How B.R.A.V.E. Human Leadership Behaviors Define Relational Leaders: Leading With Mind and Heart. https://www.thehli.com/research/

4. Audience Audit, & Human Leadership Institute. (2024, September). How B.R.A.V.E. Human Leadership Behaviors Define Relational Leaders: Leading With Mind and Heart. https://www.thehli.com/research/

5. Audience Audit, & Human Leadership Institute. (2024, September). How B.R.A.V.E. Human Leadership Behaviors Define Relational Leaders: Leading With Mind and Heart. https://www.thehli.com/research/

6. Taylor, B. (2014, July 23). Do you pass the leadership test?. Harvard Business Review. https://hbr.org/2010/08/pass-leadership-test

Chapter 9

1. Kross, E., Berman, M., Mischel, W., & Wager, T. (2011, February 22). Social rejection shares somatosensory representations …https://www.pnas.org/doi/abs/10.1073/pnas.1102693108

2. Kross, E., Berman, M., Mischel, W., & Wager, T. (2011, February 22). Social rejection shares somatosensory representations …https://www.pnas.org/doi/abs/10.1073/pnas.1102693108

3. Kross, E., Berman, M., Mischel, W., & Wager, T. (2011, February 22). Social rejection shares somatosensory representations …https://www.pnas.org/doi/abs/10.1073/pnas.1102693108

4. Suls, J. (n.d.-b). *Cognitive dissonance of Leon Festinger*. Encyclopædia Britannica. https://www.britannica.com/biography/Leon-Festinger/Cognitive-dissonance

5. Hadley, C. N. (2021, August 27). Employees are Lonelier than ever. here's how employers can help. Harvard Business Review. https://hbr.org/2021/06/employees-are-lonelier-than-ever-heres-how-employers-can-help

6. Gallo, A. (2023, February 15). What is psychological safety?. Harvard Business Review. https://hbr.org/2023/02/what-is-psychological-safety

7. Bruce, L. D., Wu, J. S., Lustig, S. L., Russell, D. W., & Nemecek, D. A. (2019). Loneliness in the United States: A 2018 National Panel Survey of demographic, structural, cognitive, and behavioral characteristics. American Journal of Health Promotion, 33(8), 1123–1133. https://doi.org/10.1177/0890117119856551

8. Audience Audit, & Human Leadership Institute. (2024, September). How B.R.A.V.E. Human Leadership Behaviors Define Relational Leaders: Leading With Mind and Heart. https://www.thehli.com/research/

9. Carr, E. W., Reese, A., Kellerman, G. R., & Robichaux, A. (2021, December 21). The value of belonging at work. Harvard Business Review. https://hbr.org/2019/12/the-value-of-belonging-at-work

10. Lewitt, S. (2022, August 24). *Is remote working fuelling a loneliness epidemic?*. theHRDIRECTOR. https://www.thehrdirector.com/features/flexible-working/remote-working-fuelling-loneliness-epidemic/

11. Carr, E. W., Reese, A., Kellerman, G. R., & Robichaux, A. (2021, December 21). The value of belonging at work. Harvard Business Review. https://hbr.org/2019/12/the-value-of-belonging-at-work

12. Carr, E. W., Reese, A., Kellerman, G. R., & Robichaux, A. (2021, December 21). The value of belonging at work. Harvard Business Review. https://hbr.org/2019/12/the-value-of-belonging-at-work

13. Carr, E. W., Reese, A., Kellerman, G. R., & Robichaux, A. (2021, December 21). The value of belonging at work. Harvard Business Review. https://hbr.org/2019/12/the-value-of-belonging-at-work

14. Audience Audit, & Human Leadership Institute. (2024, September). How B.R.A.V.E. Human Leadership Behaviors Define Relational Leaders: Leading With Mind and Heart. https://www.thehli.com/research/

15. Audience Audit, & Human Leadership Institute. (2024, September). How B.R.A.V.E. Human Leadership Behaviors Define Relational Leaders: Leading With Mind and Heart. https://www.thehli.com/research/

16. Doyle, G. (2020). Untamed. The Dial Press.

17. Croneberger, J. (2020, March 4). Council Post: Vision, mission *and purpose: The difference*. Forbes. https://www.forbes.com/councils/forbescoachescouncil/2020/03/04/vision-mission-and-purpose-the-difference/

## Chapter 10

18. Oppland, M. (2024, July 26). *8 traits of flow according to Mihaly Csikszentmihalyi*. PositivePsychology.com. https://positivepsychology.com/mihaly-csikszentmihalyi-father-of-flow/

19. Audience Audit, & Human Leadership Institute. (2024, September). How B.R.A.V.E. Human Leadership Behaviors Define Relational Leaders: Leading With Mind and Heart. https://www.thehli.com/research/

20. Audience Audit, & Human Leadership Institute. (2024, September). How B.R.A.V.E. Human Leadership Behaviors Define Relational Leaders: Leading With Mind and Heart. https://www.thehli.com/research/

## Chapter 11

1. Audience Audit, & Human Leadership Institute. (2024, September). How B.R.A.V.E. Human Leadership Behaviors Define Relational Leaders: Leading With Mind and Heart. https://www.thehli.com/research/

2. Riggio, R. (2014, January 22). What is authentic leadership? do you have it?. Psychology Today. https://www.psychologytoday.com/us/blog/cutting-edge-leadership/201401/what-is-authentic-leadership-do-you-have-it

3. Best, K. (2018, August 7). Know thyself: The philosophy of self-knowledge. UConn Today. https://today.uconn.edu/2018/08/know-thyself-philosophy-self-knowledge/

4. Audience Audit, & Human Leadership Institute. (2024, September). How B.R.A.V.E. Human Leadership Behaviors Define Relational Leaders: Leading With Mind and Heart. https://www.thehli.com/research/

## Chapter 12

1. Audience Audit, & Human Leadership Institute. (2024, September). How B.R.A.V.E. Human Leadership Behaviors Define Relational Leaders: Leading With Mind and Heart. https://www.thehli.com/research/

2. Audience Audit, & Human Leadership Institute. (2024, September). How B.R.A.V.E. Human Leadership Behaviors Define Relational Leaders: Leading With Mind and Heart. https://www.thehli.com/research/

3. Roger Bannister: First sub-four-minute mile. Guinness World Records. (n.d.). https://www.guinnessworldrecords.com/records/hall-of-fame/first-sub-four-minute-mile

4. Daley, J. (2018, March 5). Five things to know about Roger Bannister, the first person to break the 4-Minute Mile. Smithsonian.com. https://www.smithsonianmag.com/smart-news/five-things-know-about-roger-bannister-first-person-break-four-minute-mile-180968344/

5. Kotecha, T. (2021, December 15). Kathrine Switzer: First woman to officially run Boston Marathon on the iconic moment she was attacked by the race organiser. Sky Sports. https://www.skysports.com/amp/more-sports/athletics/news/29175/12475824/kathrine-switzer-first-woman-to-officially-run-boston-marathon-on-the-iconic-moment-she-was-attacked-by-the-race-organiser

6. Hamilton, E. L. (2018, June 29). Until 1972, women were prohibited from running the Boston Marathon and the first female to complete race had to hide in the bushes before starting: The vintage news. The Vintage News. https://www.thevintagenews.com/2017/12/03/boston-marathon/

7. Arguinchona, J. H. (2023, July 24). Neuroanatomy, reticular activating system. StatPearls [Internet]. https://www.ncbi.nlm.nih.gov/books/NBK549835/

Chapter 13

1. Audience Audit, & Human Leadership Institute. (2024, September). How B.R.A.V.E. Human Leadership Behaviors Define Relational Leaders: Leading With Mind and Heart. https://www.thehli.com/research/

2. Patton, L. (2020a, August 18). The Future of Leadership is empathy and companies are better for it. Entrepreneur. https://www.entrepreneur.com/leadership/the-future-of-leadership-is-empathy8212and-companies-are/354774

3. Audience Audit, & Human Leadership Institute. (2024, September). How B.R.A.V.E. Human Leadership Behaviors Define Relational Leaders: Leading With Mind and Heart. https://www.thehli.com/research/

4. 4. Audience Audit, & Human Leadership Institute. (2024, September). How B.R.A.V.E. Human Leadership Behaviors Define Relational Leaders: Leading With Mind and Heart. https://www.thehli.com/research/

5. Kirzinger, A., & Lopes, L. (2022, October 6). KFF/CNN Mental Health in America Survey . KFF. https://www.kff.org/report-section/kff-cnn-mental-health-in-america-survey-findings/

6. Rusch, H., & Bagereka, P. (2021, August 4). Ease your return-to-work anxiety. Anxiety and Depression Association of America, ADAA. https://adaa.org/learn-from-us/from-the- experts/blog-posts/consumer/ease-your-return-work-anxiety

7. Rusch, H., & Bagereka, P. (2021, August 4). Ease your return-to-work anxiety. Anxiety and Depression Association of America, ADAA. https://adaa.org/learn-from-us/from-the-experts/blog-posts/consumer/ease-your-return-work-anxiety

8. 2023 Workplace Wellness Research. Mental Health America. (2023). https://www.mhanational.org/2023-workplace-wellness-research#:~:text=In%202022%2C%2081%25%20of%20workers,78%25%20of%20respondents%20in%202021

9. Audience Audit, & Human Leadership Institute. (2024, September). How B.R.A.V.E. Human Leadership Behaviors Define Relational Leaders: Leading With Mind and Heart. https://www.thehli.com/research/

10. Landry, L. (2019, April 3). Emotional intelligence in leadership: Why it's important. Harvard Business School Business Insights . https://online.hbs.edu/blog/post/emotional-intelligence-in-leadership

11. Audience Audit, & Human Leadership Institute. (2024, September). How B.R.A.V.E. Human Leadership Behaviors Define Relational Leaders: Leading With Mind and Heart. https://www.thehli.com/research/

## Chapter 14

1. Kratz, J. (2024, May 9). *The rise of AI underscores a need for human skills*. Forbes. https://www.forbes.com/sites/juliekratz/2023/12/17/have-we-forgotten-about-human-skills-in-the-age-of-ai/?sh=213140936a7d

2. Conway, S. (2024, April 1). AI enables us to put the human back into work!. LinkedIn. https://www.linkedin.com/pulse/ai-enables-us-put-human-back-work-stephanie-conway-gytye/

3. Conway, S. (2024, April 1). AI enables us to put the human back into work!. LinkedIn. https://www.linkedin.com/pulse/ai-enables-us-put-human-back-work-stephanie-conway-gytye/

4. Roslansky, R. (2024, January 26). The ai-fueled future of work needs humans more than ever. Wired. https://www.wired.com/story/the-ai-fueled-future-of-work-needs-humans-more-than-ever/

## Chapter 16

1. Harter, J. (2024, August 1). *3 key insights into the global workplace*. Gallup.com. https://www.gallup.com/workplace/645416/key-insights-global-workplace.aspx

2. Harter, J. (2024, August 1). *3 key insights into the global workplace*. Gallup.com. https://www.gallup.com/workplace/645416/key-insights-global-workplace.aspx

3. Harter, J. (2024, August 1). *3 key insights into the global workplace*. Gallup.com. https://www.gallup.com/workplace/645416/key-insights-global-workplace.aspx

4. Knoepflmacher, D. (2024, April 4). *America's loneliness epidemic: What is to be done?* Weill Cornell Medicine. https://weillcornell.org/news/america%E2%80%99s-loneliness-epidemic-what-is-to-be-done#:~:text=In%20May%202023%2C%20the%20U.S.,Loneliness%20and%20social%20isolation%2C%20Dr.

5. Shapiro, R. M. (1995). *Wisdom of the jewish sages: A modern reading of Pirke Avot*. Bell Tower.

As you close this book, I invite you to continue the conversation and deepen your journey. If you've felt inspired, there are many ways to dive in further:

1. Explore the *Meet Them Where They Are* workbook for additional insights and growth.
2. Download our comprehensive research report on Relational Leadership
3. Discover our courses and other offerings at the Human Leadership Institute, designed to support you in building stronger, more connected relationships.

Wherever you are on your leadership journey, know we're here to walk alongside you… Because we aren't meant to do this alone.

Visit us at http://www.thehli.com/
to learn more or use the QR code below.

We will be waiting for you.
Now,
"Let's get to work."

www.ingramcontent.com/pod-product-compliance
Lightning Source LLC
LaVergne TN
LVHW051141260925
821913LV00004B/13